W9-DJK-060

The MANUFACTURERS' REPRESENTATIVE

Exemplifying the philosophy of the INDEPENDENT PROFESSIONAL SALESMAN

by

Frank Lebell

VOLUME I

HILLS-BAY PRESS
P.O. Box 5221
San Mateo, Calif. 94402

Library of Congress
Catalog Card No. 78-27599

First printing May 1971
Second printing November 1971
Third printing April 1972
Fourth printing September 1972
Fifth printing January 1974

Published by
HILLS-BAY PRESS
P.O. Box 5221
San Mateo, California 94402

Manufactured in the United States of America

To Maryan,

with love

CONTENTS

Introduction

Chapter — Page

PREFACE
AUTHOR'S VERY PERSONAL NOTE
SOME DOWN-TO-EARTH WORDS FOR THE UNINITIATED

1 BY WAY OF DEFINITION ...... with something of semantics 1
2 WHERE DO YOU GET LINES . Like, where do you get blood? 5
3 KIND OF LINES YOU WANT ...... A rep can dream, can't he? 10
4 SOLE PROPRIETORSHIP? PARTNERSHIP? INC.? LTD.? ...... Which way do you go? 19
5 DISTRIBUTOR OR INDUSTRIAL REP .. Decisions, decisions! 25
6 THE ENGINEER AS A SALESMAN .... and vice versa 28
7 APPLYING FOR A LINE ....No time to be bashful 30
8 THE SALES BOOK .... Your showcase 34
9 BOUND CATALOGS FOR CUSTOMERS ...... Forget it! Line card ideas 36
10 THE SECOND OFFICE .. 'Bye, dear – I'll try to get home early 39
11 ROUTINE FORMS AND GOLD ...... Who needs electronic data processing? 41
12 THE REP AS A CREDITOR ...... Low man on the totem pole 50
13 TRADE ASSOCIATIONS .... Antithesis of the lone wolf 54
14 SALES AGREEMENTS ... Guide lines and suggested provisions 57
15 TAKING DISTRIBUTOR INVENTORIES .... Should one? 63
16 CONVENTIONS .... and how to get lucky 65
17 AUTO STATUS .... Cadillac? Volkswagen? 68
18 THE LINE FOR THIS MONTH IS – ...... Getting the lead out 70
19 THE THREE-CENT PENCIL .... Last of the big spenders 72
20 ELEGY TO THE EXPEDITER .... a poem 74
21 YOUR IMAGE .... Touching up the wrinkles 76

Chapter Page

22 SELF-CONSCIOUSNESS IS A CURSE
...... Dissolve it with five words 80

23 BUYING HOURS .. Observing them leaves lots of time for golf 87

24 BY-PASS THE BUYER .... It's a good trick if you can 90

25 ON PLAYING SANTA CLAUS
......Must you advertise your competitor? 93

26 STORY OF A TOOTHACHE .... A fulfilling experience 95

27 SECRETARIES .... Enter sexcess; exit success! 97

28 PENNY PINCHERS .... A hundred pennies still equal a dollar 102

29 CALLS WITH YOUR SALESMAN .... Surprise, surprise! 104

30 LETTERS TO PRINCIPALS .... The long and short of it 107

31 SALES MANAGERS .... It takes all kinds 111

32 THE QUOTA .... A blessing in disguise 121

33 BIG VS. SMALL CUSTOMERS .... Is there a preference? 125

34 PUBLICITY .... National advertising for free 128

35 ETHICS; LAW OF THE JUNGLE ..... and termination clauses 130

36 CUSTOMER CREDIT .... The rep makes like D & B 134

37 THE REP AS A DISTRIBUTOR
...... How do you divide one by two? 137

38 THE HIRING SALESMEN PROBLEM
...... What price "associate"? 141

39 YOUR WEAK SPOTS .... A way of self-analysis 146

40 THE BRANCH OFFICE . How far does a rubber band stretch? 148

41 IS IT BETTER TO BE BIGGER? Small lines, big lines and nets 150

42 COFFEE BREAK . Odds and ends to think about between sips 155

43 SO YOU WANT TO GROW
.... I'm not hungry –
I just want to get rich, that's all 161

44 FUTURE OF THE REP PROFESSION
...... Comes the revolution –! 165

45 ANTICIPATING RETIREMENT
...... For the oddball who prefers
fishing, golfing and homelife
to sales managers, expediters and secretaries 172

PREFACE

The manufacturers' representative has come a long way in the span of one man's lifetime. He has left behind the belittling term, "peddler," that anachronism of the radio crystal set era. By his own efforts, he has managed to establish himself as an important factor in the marketing of industrial and technological developments.

In his modern status as a professional independent salesman, he is looked to as a consultant, a marketing authority, a branch of the company whom he represents. He is the key to the interlocking interests of buyer and supplier. As such, the ramifications of his services extend far beyond selling. How did he get that way?

To attain proficiency as a "rep" transcends the scope of college training. He has had to acquire his expertise the lone hard way. Ergo, "The Manufacturers' Representative" is a pragmatic work, making available to the later comer *the laser of hindsight* as it is focussed on experiences of those who have already come over the road. Just as projections of the computer depend on past events, so may the data compiled herein be utilized in programming the travels ahead.

Taken as a handbook, "The Manufacturers' Representative" makes no pretense of being the final word. The rep may be confronted with special circumstances which only his own resourcefulness can resolve. But in the sense of a basic and advanced course for both the beginner and the already established rep, the book is at all times philosophically realistic in presenting the "how-to" principles of successful manufacturers' representation. The language is blunt, outspoken, reflecting the kind of world we live in today.

In the final analysis, admittedly no man is going to learn the business only by reading about it – any more than one can learn to swim simply by reading how. But for the man poised for his initial plunge, for the man in turbulence already lashing out in his endeavors to go faster and further, the intent of "The Manufacturers' Representative" is to help ease the necessity for doing it "the hard way."

The rest is up to the individual himself.

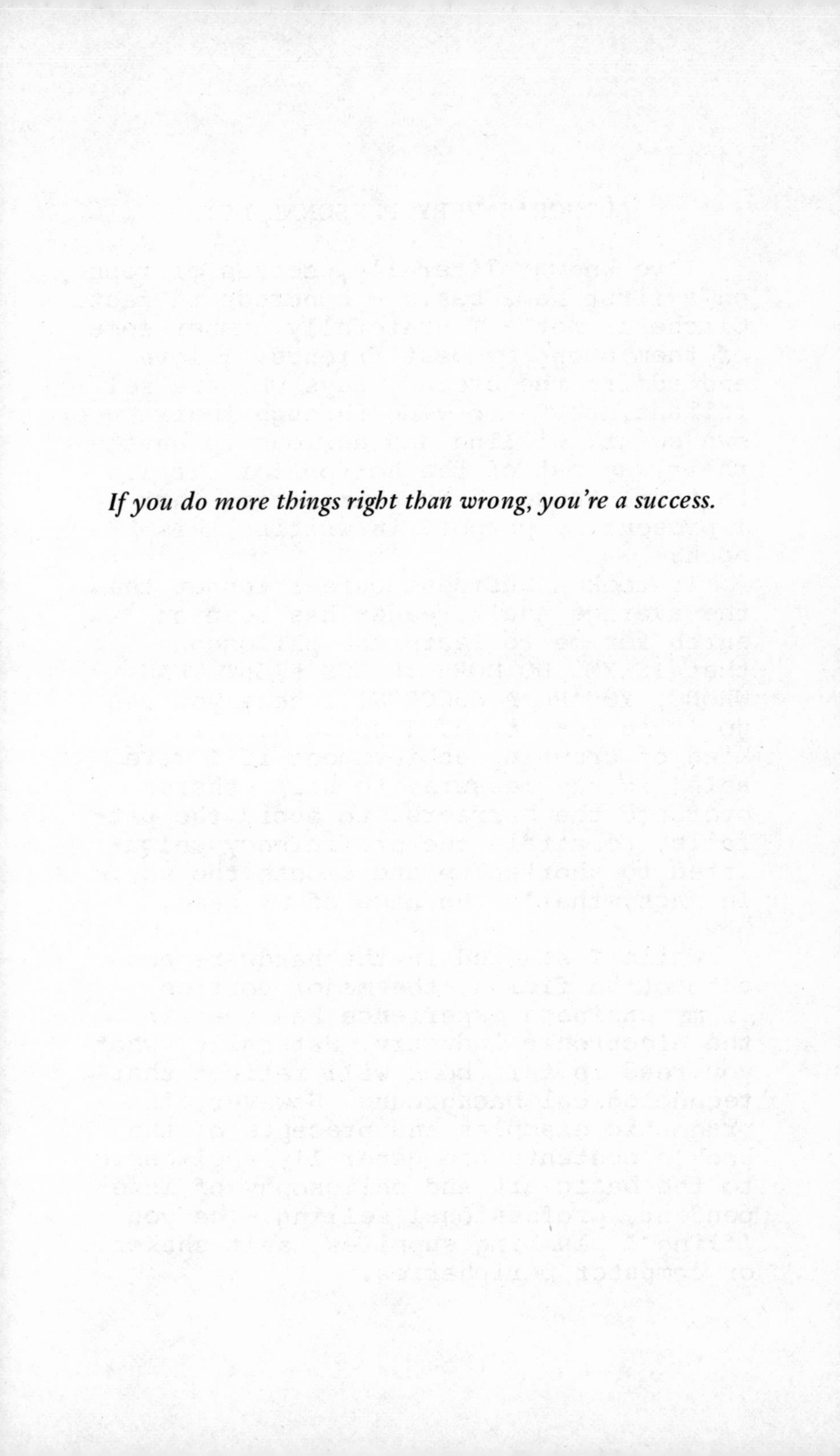

If you do more things right than wrong, you're a success.

AUTHOR'S VERY PERSONAL NOTE

I've known, literally, scores of reps on a first name basis - hundreds in fact. Cliche or not - I gratefully number some of them among my best friends. I love and admire the breed - guys who are self-reliant, ready to wade through their own sweat, willing and anxious to battle their way out of the hoi-polloi. It is to them, those hardy characters, that I present my purpose in writing this book:

It took a business career longer than the average adult reader has been on earth for me to learn the philosophy that IF YOU DO MORE THINGS RIGHT THAN WRONG, YOU'RE A SUCCESS! I hope you can do it in less time. I would deem it a kind of crowning achievement if I were able, in any measure, to help others overcome the barriers, to avoid the pitfalls, to attain the proficiency calculated to shorten up and smooth the way. In fact, that's the name of my game.

While I started in the hardware and automotive fields, the major portion of my business experience has been in the electronic industry. Naturally, what you read in this book will reflect that technological background. However, the pragmatic examples and precepts of the book's contents are generally applicable to the basic art and philosophy of independent, professional selling - be your ''line'' plumbing supplies, salt shakers or computer peripheries.

Granted, in this world, nobody has the DEFINITIVE answers to anything. Being human, you and I may differ on the merits of spending money for trips to the moon all the way down to debating whether or not that expensive electric eraser your secretary wants for her typewriter is really a time-saving assist to efficiency, or just a concession to keeping her happy. At many points, the book is deliberately provocative in that it sets out the pros and cons of given situations, rights and wrongs stemming from the real life experience of many reps - yours to study as guideposts for doing it YOUR way.

The rep business has been good to me. I hope it does at least as much for you, if not more. And if this book helps, in even a small degree - well, as indicated above, that's why it was written.

Good luck!

Frank Lebell

San Mateo, California

SOME DOWN-TO-EARTH WORDS FOR THE UNINITIATED

The profession of representing manufacturers in a selling capacity has all the outward appearance of simplicity. Many of those who have dealt for years with "reps" will rattle off, knowingly, "There's nothing to it. All it requires is a few lines, a supply of catalogs, a car and a gift of gab." With sniffing envy, they point to the rep's obvious affluence – the nice car he drives, his modish attire, the insouciance with which he picks up the drinks and luncheon tab. Working hours are short; after all, the rep can only call on purchasing departments during regular buying hours which, as everyone knows, are very limited. It's a cinch life!

Not – quite!

To be a manufacturers' representative is a tremendously rewarding occupation but, to begin with, it is suitable only for a certain type of man. If I may repeat my favorite analogy: the man born to be a rep is one who, let's say, might be left alone in a vast, empty desert, with only his hands and wits to help him survive. The next time you came along, you would find him set up in the business of selling desert rocks and fauna as souvenirs to the tourists passing by.

Along with resourcefulness, to be a rep calls especially for a bottomless supply of intestinal fortitude. Knowing the ease with which a qualified man can fill a well paying job, with its unionized hours, pensions, comforting fringe benefits and a pre-determined future, the rep must be willing to face up to the responsibilities, the vicissitudes, the sacrifices and hard work devolving upon the one who makes the decisions. It calls for spirit, the squared-up shoulders of one who believes in himself, that what others have done, he can do. The faint-hearted one had best eschew the rep business and remain a cog in some corporate machine. In this world of realities, "the cowards never start, the weak die by the way."

It's a great life being a rep – but, if you think it's easy, forget it!

1
BY WAY OF DEFINITION

– with something of semantics

The Marketeer

The awkward length of the cumbersome "manufacturers' representative" is commonly (and herein) compressed to "rep." Considering the rep's widespread functions in marketing, use of a word like, say, "marketeer," might serve as meaningful while presenting lingual facility. Be that as it may, in legal jargon, he is described as an "independent sales contractor." As such, he operates his own business at his own expense. Remuneration is based solely on commission. In a proscribed territory, he markets the products of non-competitive manufacturers ("manufacturers" in the usual meaning but also including variations, such as service organizations and companies who have no proprietary products but fabricate according to the customer's specifications).*

The advanced rep's approach to selling is that of a professional. He is an authority in his field. He looks out for the principal's interests in all respects. He keeps the principal aware of territorial conditions, acts as a consultant, advises of circumstances arising favorable or otherwise, of customer credit situations. While observing policies of those represented, he nevertheless employs his own methods in promoting sale of the principal's products.

Legally, and in the popular idiom, the rep functions as "his own boss" – with all that expression entails in the way of responsibility. It is in this larger sense of self-dependence

---

*Note that throughout this book, use of the generic abbreviation "rep" for the term "manufacturers' representative" refers equally to "sales agent".

that the rep exemplifies one who has extricated himself from the cogs and wheels of the corporate machine. Apart from possible monetary rewards, he derives that head-lifting, shoulder-bracing satisfaction of a man who can look upon something which he, himself, creates. In the fulfillment of being "his own boss," the rep demonstrates a triumph of the human spirit over the sheep-like, enforced submissiveness of the organization man.

Agent vs. Representative

Sometimes the word "agent" is interchanged loosely with the word "representative." The term "agent" is commonly applied to so many diversified occupations that defining it precisely is difficult. Nevertheless, there are differences between "agent" and "representative," however shadowy, with perhaps legal implications. "Agent" tends to indicate one charged with specific duties, methods, etc., as in the case of employees – which is contrary to the free-lance, independent character of the rep's functions.

It is true that the "yellow pages" include a column headed "manufacturers' agents" but this is a broad, general grab-bag. Preferably, for example, the electronic rep should be listed separately under "Electronic Manufacturers' Representatives," thereby more particularly distinguishing his trade classification. The same goes for any major industry.

Distinctions of this kind should be observed because of the responsibility factor.* For the same reason, it is important that the sales contract include properly worded provisions concerning warranties. It would be well to set forth that the rep is in nowise accountable for the manufacturers' implied or promised performance of his products, that this is solely the manufacturers' responsibility, particularly significant in view of the increasing frequency of dissatisfied consumer lawsuits.

---

*The rep is advised to consult his attorney for explanations of the difference between being designated as "representative" or "agent."

Jobber vs. Distributor

One of the most common errors in business speech is the mistaken assumption that the words "*jobber*" and "*distributor*" are synonymous. Common usage has blurred their original meanings, perhaps to the puzzlement of the newcomer desirous of conforming with correct trade terminology.

"*Jobber*" is defined as one who deals in intermittent, random, odd "job lots" of merchandise. In electronics, he came into prominent existence in radio's early years, when financial distress or discontinuance of models led to devastating "dumping" practices. In turn, this created the "salvage" class of operators, to be commonly referred to as "jobbers." As manufacturing methods and policies improved, the industry settled down to merchandising through so-called "regular" avenues. The sensational "limited quantity, one-shot" dealer broadened into or was supplanted by the merchant engaged in conventional re-sale of widely varied brands, handling more or less standardized goods, to become the typical wholesale supply house of today.

"*Distributor*" is defined as one dealing regularly in a specifically classified line or product, rather than haphazard "special buys" – very likely in some versions of franchised operation. He might resell at retail, at wholesale, or both, in a proscribed territory, depending on the terms of his appointment by the manufacturer. This is why the rep and manufacturer should avoid the use of "jobber," confining themselves to "distributor" in the wording of franchising a given line.

Today, both expressions are used frequently, with little discrimination, to describe widely differing kinds of business – especially the word "distributor." Except where legalities might pertain (as in franchising, for example), the commercial world is seldom concerned with pedanticisms. But evidently the distinctive "exclusive" charisma accorded the word "distributor" and the somewhat unsavory connotations of the "dumping" period led to favoring the term "distributor" over "jobber." In any event, with "distributor" now appearing to be the more popular term, and "jobber" being a telltale revelation of the speaker's age, this book's author bows to the glories of progress and will hereinafter carry on with the word "distributor."

2
WHERE DO YOU GET LINES?

Like, where do you get blood?

As in the case of the merchant's inventory on his shelves, LINES are the rep's stock in trade.* But there are no wholesalers of "lines," no warehouse supplies, no specific source from which to obtain your stock. How do you get lines?

Good question! One might analogize: where does the life-giving blood come from that courses through one's veins? Well, as is proved by the thousands of rep firms existing across the country, there are ways. Let's take a look at the more common procedures – some simple and obvious, others more sophisticated, but none at all in order of importance because one way can be just as likely as another:

Trade publications are good. Manufacturers seeking representation very often advertise their requirements. (You would do well to subscribe to several trade publications. They can be illuminating and educational in more ways than one).

Advertise yourself in trade publications. Word your ad to include the category of products in which you are interested, describe your personnel, the territory you cover, etc. (See the chapter headed, "Applying for lines.")

You might read of a new manufacturer starting up, or of one who is expanding from a limited territory to nation-wide,

---

*TIME is capital you invest – but that you got for free, of course, inherited from your parents.

holding some possibilities for your interest. Study ads describing products suitable for your activities; after ascertaining that the manufacturer is not already represented in your territory (to be discussed later), direct an enquiry to him about the possibility of representing him.

Trade associations are, in a number of ways, prolific sources for acquiring lines. Some, such as the Electronic Representatives Association, solicit and compile data from manufacturers looking for reps and distribute the information among their memberships. (At conventions, ERA posts notices of such manufacturers' requirements in the Association's booth, as well as making periodical mailings which list "lines available.")

Mingle with your fellow reps. In general conversation, they will speak of lines "open" for representation. Many reps, long established, receive enquiries from manufacturers in which they are not personally interested – they are glad to pass these on to newcomers. (Don't be cynical about this. In his earlier years, this writer had occasion to note that many of his lines had been acquired originally by referrals from other reps. I can gratefully testify that it does happen.)

By train or plane, afoot or horseback, by all means attend the conventions! Go into hock, if need be – but be there. Don't allow the weary cynicism of old-time reps about conventions deceive you – trade shows are of paramount importance. New manufacturers exhibit at shows – it is a traditional time and place for those seeking representatives. In circulating about the show, keep your eyes and ears open. Be sure to engage other reps in conversation – news about lines "open" travels rapidly across the floor at conventions.

The customers already on your calling list can be a significant source for recommending lines to you. They are among the first to hear of terminations. Sometimes they are buying products direct from a factory for which there is no local representative. Let friendly buyers know you would be interested in acquiring "just one more line."

Fair game and a likely target is to solicit the line of the manufacturer who is employing "direct" so-called representatives (i.e., salaried salesmen). You have a tremendous array of logical, persuasive reasoning at your command.

Start with his selling expense. Challenge him to compare the *total* cost of selling "direct" with what it would cost him if he were paying you on a commission basis. You can relieve him immediately of the need for shelling out money to salesmen when business isn't coming in. You offer the coverage and extensive services of a sales-trained staff at no cost to him; he pays only an always-fixed percentage on business actually placed in his hands. If his business is sizable, your availability as a regional sales manager is offered for free. The burdens of hiring and training sales engineers are borne by you, as well as the costs of "fringe benefits," thus effecting another substantial saving for him.

Stress the fact that your other lines bring you into far-flung markets, into corners which are off-beat for his direct salesmen, thereby digging up prospects of which he would know nothing otherwise. Impressive is the fact that you are in business for yourself, that you have *got* to work harder in order to keep your business going, that there is no similar impelling factor on the hired hand who, in the normal course of events, can get by with just ordinary effort. Point out that he is relieved of worries about continual turnover of help, about goldbrickers, about chiseling and padding of expense accounts.

A recent development for initiating representation arrangements has been the introduction of a kind of third party, with the announced purpose of bringing together prospective principals and representatives. Briefly described: this procedure starts with the rep receiving a mailing asking if he is interested in acquiring new lines. He is urged to fill out a questionnaire enclosed, calling for various details about his activities. He is told many lines will be made available to him. The solicitation points out there will be no charge made to the rep for this service.

Those promoting the proposition advertise themselves to manufacturers as a source for any requiring representation, based on their files built up from these rep questionnaires. In short: this is a two-way street operation, quite similar to that of an employment agency.

How kindly reps will take to having to deal with the complications of still another element in seeking lines, is a moot question. Otherwise, the process is still too new for comment, one way or the other. For some, it is evident that this might be a way of getting a crack at lines open of which they might not otherwise become aware. A sales manager may be simply taking this course as a means of narrowing down applicants for his line to the most desirable, and is willing to pay an "agency" to do this chore for him.

Expose yourself! Let people *know* you are looking for lines. You don't have to be diffident about this. It is commonplace knowledge that *every* rep, no matter how big, how affluent, is always on the lookout for desirable new lines, so why not you? I once heard the manager of an insurance company say, while speaking to a group of trainees, "Tell five people a day, every day, that you are in the insurance business, at the same time handing each one your card. By the law of averages, just doing that alone will make you a living out of the insurance business." The same thinking holds good for the rep – the more you let it be known that you are looking, the more likely you are to be remembered when something comes up of possible interest to you.

At this point, I must interject one "Don't." You can tell

everybody you are seeking lines but don't look to your sales managers for help in this regard. Does this strike you as curious? For example: you've done a good job for a factory. The sales manager has let you know he is very pleased with you. Your relations are most cordial. You know he meets frequently with other sales managers, in association meetings and in one way or another. Might he not happen to hear of a sales manager looking for a rep in your territory? And since he feels so friendly toward you, wouldn't it seem logical that he bring up your name as a prospect for the line?

Forget it! He won't!

It is a cardinal principle for the sales manager to absorb, to take for himself all of the rep's time he can possibly garner. He is reluctant to see you taking on another line, particularly an important one, because he sees it as detracting from time and attention given to *his* line.

Is that selfish of him? Well – business of shrugging the shoulders – he's got *his* job to protect, hasn't he?

This much he *will* do. Assuming you are already negotiating for a line, he might give you at least a perfunctory recommendation in the event he is favorable to you, if you have seen fit to offer his name as reference to the prospective new principal. Some might be even enthusiastic in giving you a good sendoff. But don't think of a sales manager as a logical *initial* source for recommending new lines to you.

Publicity is an indirect but possible factor in acquiring lines – to be discussed more fully later. There are other random ways in which you will find lines available – too isolated and varied, and stemming from your own particular circumstances, to take up here. Just remember this: among the many thousands of manufacturers in this country, only a fraction are ordinarily represented in a given territory. There are innumerable possibilities. The problem is not too horrendous – the *real* problem is how to select *good* lines. For that important subject, we will need another chapter.

3
KIND OF LINES YOU WANT

A rep can dream, can't he?

Assuming availability, the category of lines you elect to handle will depend on numerous factors having to do with your temperament and background, your social aptitudes, technological requirements, a variety of circumstantial detail and, basically, your judgment of the potential market for the lines to be considered. Of these, the extent to which one is technically qualified, frequently comes to the fore.

It goes without saying that to handle complex fabrications such as are characteristic of the electronic industry – the solid state devices, the modules, the instrumentation systems and the like, makes technical understanding of the engineering involved absolutely mandatory. But there are many products which require little more than familiarity with mechanical and/or electrical fundamentals. Even the fast-expanding field of computer peripheries offers so-called "soft-ware" items which can be sold without knowing how to operate a computer.

There is no end to the world's proliferation of new products. Lines vary from fantastically complex to the simplicity of children's toys. Some call for the technically oriented salesman; others are much more dependent on personality traits, on the ability to socialize, to make personal friends and, above all, selling technique. Where you fit in is up to you.

With due allowance for occasional exceptions, try to avoid the highly specialized product lines, particularly the "one item" variety. The market for one special item is bound to be limited. It usually calls for more than normal sales effort; sufficient compensation is questionable. Most reps have, at one time or another, become enamored with some new, ingenious watchamatronic and have undertaken to introduce it to the trade, with disappointing results. All too frequently, such appealing items are originated by comparatively new manufacturers, with limited finances. Not being able to back up the rep with good advertising, with promotion tools, it is the rep who has to carry the ball, who has to wait a long, long time before decent size commission checks come through. The game is seldom worth it, even though, once in a blue moon, there is such a thing as running across a "sleeper."

Don't be negative but look with a judicious eye at so-called "contract engineering" lines. This refers to the "manufacturer" who may be very well equipped to turn out fine, usable products but has no proprietary items. In lieu of standardized, catalog products, he describes extensive plant facilities and technical know-how. He offers to make such-and-such "to the customers' specifications." Very often, he lists a number of impressive, nationally known names whom he refers to as customers (without necessarily specifying how much business he actually got from them!)

Don't turn down this type of line summarily; it might have good possibilities, but give its special kind of drawbacks plenty of consideration. Servicing such principals usually calls for keeping a good supply of aspirin on hand. First, you have to beat the bushes, searching out those isolated prospects who might buy something this manufacturer is equipped to make. Special tooling to fill an order might be required. The problem arises: who pays for the tooling and who owns it afterwards – leading to the likelihood the rep gets no commission on the tooling (which can be a major amount of the transaction).

Assuming you get what appears to be a good order; comes the drawings, the specifications which may or may not be clear and complete, to be followed by numerous back-and-forth changes while the deal is in transit. Whether or not the usual commission rates are generous enough to compensate for the extra effort entailed in promoting such a line, is debatable. In short: you would do well to think hard about the desirability of playing this three-handed game of ping-pong with you in the middle!

Then we have the type of manufacturer who has either poor literature or perhaps none at all. He explains that they are "just working on a new catalog" but is vague as to the exact time for its publication. He may also toss out something about while they are not advertising at the moment, they "expect" to start a big campaign, again at some undetermined future date.

Aside from the all-important need for a good catalog which any tyro in business is aware of, the lack of this basic selling tool *has* to mean this manufacturer either doesn't know his business or he can't afford to pay for the printing. Which means, the matter of when and whether or not the rep is going to receive any commissions due becomes a subject for dubious speculation. Beware!

Don't be afraid to take on a line with which some previous rep has had little or no success – at least, not for that reason. There can be many explanations for his severance of relations with that manufacturer. Perhaps that rep didn't know where those particular products were bought in quantities. He could have been just generally incompetent. Or he might have decided to unload this line in order to make room for another he considered more important. Perhaps it was (and frequently is) a clash of personalities between the rep and the sales manager.

By all means, try to ascertain by checking with the

previous rep himself just why he parted company with the outfit. You might be told the factory had shortcomings when it came to paying commissions, that they were not alert to or capable of meeting competitive conditions. It is also possible that while the faults of which he complains may have been as he describes them, perhaps the factory has taken steps to correct them. Naturally, the former rep will make explanations of a face-saving nature – you've got to take what he gives you with plenty of salt!

Additional factors having influence on the choice of lines will show up as you read through other chapters.

What are the attributes of a desirable line? The order of importance will vary with individual circumstances, but they generally include most of the following considerations:

1. Usefulness of the products – widespread or limited.
2. Pricing, especially as compared to competition.
3. Manufacturer's responsibility: financial, years in business, kind of personnel, past history in the trade, overall reputation.
4. Rate and fixed date for paying commissions.
5. Split commission situations; how handled.
6. Plant facilities; technical assistance; frequency of trips into rep's territory.
7. Availability of good literature, samples.
8. Distributor or Industrial oriented; detailed programs. Efficient, attractive packaging.
9. Delivery schedules and practices.
10. Advertising programs; exhibits at Shows.
11. Sales Volume.
12. Termination period.

Some time ago, an article by the writer entitled, "A Rep Can Dream, Can't He?" was published in ERA's "The Representor." By permission, it is reproduced here, not just for laughs but because, in ironical form, it depicts an ideal line. In a way, it is a kind of recap, the very epitome of the business, from a rep's point of view:

A REP CAN DREAM, CAN'T HE?

The scene: *a sales manager, chatting with a rep, asks if this rep would be interested in taking on his line.*

REP: Sorry – got all the lines I can handle right now. In fact, I'm figuring on dropping a couple.
SM: Perhaps you can suggest someone else who might – ?
REP: Sure – glad to help out. I know one or two fellows who are hungry.
SM: Well, I dunno. I'm as big-hearted as the next one, but – you see – unfortunately a hungry man can be desperate. There's always the chance that such a man is liable to play both ends against the middle. Of course, there might be exceptions –
REP: Oh, I suppose it depends. Anyway, just give me the main facts about your line and I'll pass the info along.
SM: Okay – let's start with our catalog, the most important tool we have for our reps. It describes our facilities, but it goes light on the blurb stuff. The products are described in detail: functions, mounting directions, clear pictures, line drawings, dimensions, material data and so on. It's completely indexed. Costs us a fortune, believe me!
REP: Yeah – I've heard that before! So how many times does the rep have to beg for these 'objets d'art" before he gets a supply?
SM: He just has to tell us once how many he can use. Each edition, he gets all he asks for – fast, off the press. And more, whenever he needs them. Why, that's our best advertisement! We want it wherever our kind of products are used – and we figure the rep knows where that should be. And if he doesn't ask for catalogs, we know he isn't working the line.

REP: You got quotas?
SM: Forget it! Reps are individualists, per se. In my book, the man who elects to become a rep is an aggressive character, a self-starter. If he needs prodding, he shouldn't be in the rep business.
REP: So you just sit back and wait for the rep to send you whatever orders he happens to get –
SM: Wait a minute! On the contrary! We do provide a special incentive for the rep who does extra well by us in promoting our business.
REP: How?
SM: We relate each year to totals of preceding years. If, in the current year, he increases our business substantially –
REP: You award him a pretty plaque, I suppose?
SM: Hell, no! Our reps can furnish their own wall decorations. For a given annual increase in our business, he receives a bonus check – cold cash – over and above his regular commissions.
REP: You're becoming interesting. How about – shall we call it – conventioneering?
SM: I know what you're getting at. We are only too well aware that convention visitors can see reps any old time – that they want to talk with factory people. We turn out!
REP: So where does the rep fit in?
SM: We want him looking around the convention floor or the hotels for important customers, to steer them into our booth. We expect him to alert us to key individuals for special attention. He should visit other booths – to see what our competitors are showing, to broaden his familiarity with the state of the art by studying all the exhibitits. He should get together with reps from other territories and exchange ideas, pick up new methods –
REP: I'm finding all this hard to believe! How about that dirty word, communications?
SM: I know how anxiously a rep waits for answers to his questions and what depends on his getting them. Believe me

– we shoot them out fast – and we're not afraid to use the phone or wires if our rep indicates immediate replies required.
REP: You always keep your delivery promises, I suppose.
SM: Are you kidding? We're human, too! Certainly, we fall down once in a while. *Our* suppliers may delay us for materials, machines break down, or whatever. *But* – when that happens, we notify the rep so that he can advise the customer. That anticipates the wild, expensive expediting and forestalls the customer getting on his ear. He generally accepts the delay with good grace because we took the time and trouble to let him know beforehand that we're concerned about him. It turns an ill wind into some good. We have found that a sincere apology *before* trouble starts, can be an excellent good will builder.
REP: You seem to have an unusual understanding of what a rep needs in the way of cooperation from his principals.
SM: Well, I was a rep myself for a number of years.
REP: Ah, so! That explains it! Incidentally, what do you do about field trips?
SM: Regularly, once or twice a year, we come into every rep's territory – and at any time in between if a situation seems to call for it. We issue a continual flow of bulletins containing information about new products, good ideas some one rep has come up with that might be useful in other territories, helpful technical suggestions, new or novel uses for our products, and so on. We're always trying to educate our reps for mutual advantage.
REP: I suppose you send your reps batches of leads once in a while?
SM: No "batches." And not, "once in a while." Every lead we receive goes out to the rep soon as we get it! If we wait for an accumulation – by the time we get them, by the time they are forwarded to the rep for follow-up, the prospect has forgotten why he inquired in the first place. No sir – most leads should be acted on while they're still fresh! And an-

other thing: if the lead calls for supplying literature, for the same reason, we don't wait for the rep to do it – *we* send the inquirer the literature and let the rep know. Nor do we neglect to include the rep's name, address and phone number when we address the inquirer.

REP: Do you ask for a report back on each and every lead you send out?

SM: Of course not. We know all about piling up extra time-consuming paperwork on a man when he should be out selling. But we do assume the rep realizes how costly it is to obtain these leads, and uses them to advantage. If not, we get ourselves a new rep.

REP: Are all your reps trade association members?

SM: Absolutely! I'm aware the rep is an "independent contractor" but that doesn't mean he has to be a lone wolf. A rep should realize the importance of partaking in joint efforts to uphold and raise industry standards. If he disregards working with others for the common good, of cooperating with other trade associations, we just don't want that kind representing us.

REP: I'm sure I'm dreaming, but it's fun. Go on! All this – and you pay a commission, too, maybe?

SM: Let me put it this way: we want all of a rep's time that we can get. So, we've worked up a little scheme whereby we *seduce* him into working extra hard for us – such as, for instance, making repeated calls-back on our prospects in the face of discouragement because it's a matter of national statistics that three-fourths of all sales are closed after the fifth call. We get him to use his time on the phone, too, for extra-special follow-ups. We find him making his own mailings in our behalf for that personal touch with the people whom he knows better than we do. We look for reports on market changes, on what our competitors are doing, suggestions for new products –

REP: H'mmmm . . . And by just what cunning do you accomplish this act of seduction?

SM: Oh, it's not too difficult, really. We simply pay a high enough commission rate to warrant his getting out and working like hell for us.
REP: Look, quick – before I wake up – where's your contract? Sign me up!
SM: But you said –
REP: The hell with what I said! I want to get on your team! You're the kind of sales manager a rep dreams about!
SM: Well, fine. In that case – I have a few questions to ask *you*! Now, as to *your* operation–

The alarm clock rings.

CURTAIN

4
SOLE PROPRIETORSHIP? PARTNERSHIP? INC.? LTD.?

Which way do you go?

First, let's briefly recap the more-or-less standardized forms for engaging in commercial enterprise. I suppose in just about every case, being the sole proprietor of a business is probably the major attraction that draws a man to the rep business. He's tired of kowtowing to depersonalized, corporate "management" for his livelihood, he's an independent spirit, he has ideas of his own which he wants to try.

It's a simple way to get into business. Practically no formalities. All requirements and decisions are yours to carry out in splendid solitude, where you can be impervious to perhaps well-meaning but gratuitous kibitzers. In your office, away from the one you love and cherish dearly, who dares give you an argument? As has been said, "God made the world in one week, and even had a day to rest up – but that's because there was no one around to interfere."

The partnership form has some decided advantages particularly suitable for carrying on a rep business. Not only are efforts immediately doubled but the old adage about two heads being better than one has much merit when applied to rep operations (provided they are not both on one pair of shoulders!)

Partnerships, too, are easy to set up. It can even be done verbally, with a handshake, although that would be mistake number one. (Clasped hands might lead to a serious version of Indian arm wrestling, wherein inevitably someone has to be the loser!) Some form of written contract, drawn by an attorney should be in effect from the start.

The trend is for most rep operations to be incorporated, even when the business is owned, for all practical purposes, by one man. According to a recent trade survey, the ratio of rep firms incorporated runs about three-and-one-third to one of the other forms. Such popularity would seem to indicate this as the best way to go. Perhaps it is. However, businessmen have a way of slavishly following in the footsteps of their contemporaries, without always exploring the possible preferences of other routes. The most frequently advanced purpose of incorporating is that only one's limited interest in the corporation can be held liable in the event serious obligation is incurred. It is a belief not always warranted. Ask your attorney about the legal fraternity's ways of "piercing the veil," an allusion to the assumptions of the layman in this regard. There are other, and perhaps better reasons, for entering into the corporate form of doing business.

Another possibility, not so widely used in this country, but presenting some advantages of both the partnership and the corporation is, "Limited." This could be a desirable arrangement, assuming certain special circumstances are present. See what your attorney thinks.

Partnerships

In this writer's opinion, the usual cynicism with which the partnership form of business is dismissed, is not altogether justified. The individualistic character of the rep business should not forego the decided advantages of two individuals working together in a common cause. Liken it to a man lifting a long piece of lumber. How difficult, how he must strain to do it alone, and how much easier it becomes when two men take hold and each lifts one end.

Like everything else, the subject has its pros and cons. It's commonplace to dismiss the subject of partnerships with a dogmatic "they never work out," but that isn't necessarily true. Some do, and most successfully. It can very well be worth thinking about for the man contemplating something more than a "one man operation." The first man could supply abilities which the other lacks but which are offset by the skills of the other. One could have, say, the technical knowledge which is so important in many categories, while the other might be better in selling technique. You present the appeal to principals of *two owners* working sincerely for the good of all concerned. One can be more effective when it comes to those all-important "factory relations" than another. When one is out of town, someone reliable is left "taking care of the store." The knotty problems, the difficult decisions, can be discussed intimately, freely, without need for concealing applicable facts.

There are many beneficial aspects of partnership arrangements.

A common, generalizing explanation for partnerships not working out well is, "they didn't get along with each other." That is meaningless. Why didn't they get along? For one reason, in all too many cases, they shouldn't have joined forces in the first place. Application of a reasonable amount of understanding human nature would have foreseen the doom of the partnership before it got started. For example: an outstanding probability for trouble and one of the most common mistakes made is when two men join forces because they are *similar* in likes and dislikes, in temperament, in personality. Paradoxical as it may seem, in just those factors that make two men good personal friends may lie the very reasons why they should *not* embark upon a mutual business enterprise.

If both have the same aptitudes and similar weaknesses, the advantage is lost of one having strength where the other is weak. If both have vigorous, aggressive personalities, good for getting business, therein lies the potential for clashing with each other. Numerous instances arise of chores disagreeable to both; the evasion of one, making it necessary that the other "take care of it," is only a random example of possible disgruntlement and friction when both men are too similar in likes and dislikes.

And, of course, there is another very important condition to keep in mind when contemplating partnership. Each partner becomes 100% liable for the business obligations of the other. The word "business" is very elastic in this connection. One partner could be taking a factory visitor out for dinner and theater. He has an accident. If a lawsuit follows, the "business" aspect is sure to be brought out and the other partner becomes equally responsible. Again: one partner may have no tangible, personal assets outside of the business. The other has. The assets of the "other" can be seized upon when the penniless partner incurs a "business" liability.

The old magnet principle, that opposite poles attract and similar poles repel is applicable but, a successful partnership must include this condition:

In every enterprise involving more than one person, there can be only one leader. Though we euphemize with expressions like administration, management and so on, what it comes down to is, in their mutual interests, one must allow the other to be "front" man for both. As in marriage, each partner must recognize and accept a divergence of functions, but with the one backing up the other. (Pursuing that same analogy, one might say the main difference between living with a good partner and living with a good wife is sex.)

The give-and-take, the need for tolerance of human frailty, are nowhere so evident as in a business relationship because, basic to it all, the godalmighty dollar is at stake. Two fellows *can* get together and form a mutually profitable enterprise or they can wind up in a togethermess.

To sum up: in a partnership form of business, the odds favoring success are not the greatest but the advantages are sufficient to make consideration of the risks very much worthwhile. What *are* you sure of in this life?

Incorporation

While I have been involved in the formation of several corporations in my time, I make no pretensions of expertise in these matters. Your accountant may tell you it's a simple process and even offer to save you money by doing it for you. Don't! Your best bet is an attorney specializing in the intricacies of incorporating and, especially, the ensuing tax situation.

A good attorney will question your motives in desiring incorporation. Assuming that more than one person is involved in ownership of the business, he might suggest that, instead, it would be less complicated and cost less money to draw up a contract between you, with perhaps a decided savings on taxes. Could very well be, and deserves full exploration.

However, it is difficult to forget that seldom was drawn a contract by an attorney that some other attorney couldn't break. Furthermore, in view of the average man's difficulties with formal language, ensuing misunderstandings of complex legal terminology can lead to serious consequences.

Attorneys find this quite amusing in their smug familiarity with stock certificates but, from the layman's standpoint, that beautifully engraved piece of paper fascinates. It represents tangibility in hand, a commodity, a physical thing of specific value, something he can readily understand like a product that can be bought and sold across a counter. For practical purposes, it can function as remuneration to employees much more impressive than promises. Above all, it provides facility, a kind of "mechanics" for carrying out the making of an employee into a recognized owner in the business, as is discussed further under other chapters. In this writer's mind, that last alone makes the incorporation form of business the most desirable.

As a parting word in re forms of business operation, a subject from which it is all too human to shrink is, what happens when the owner dies insofar as tax on his estate is concerned? If you haven't already done so, by all means check with your attorney as to IRS treatment of your income when it comes to taxing your estate. Note: I refer specifically to *income* – not tangible assets.

5
DISTRIBUTOR OR INDUSTRIAL REP

Decisions, decisions!

The phenomenal expansion of modern industry has brought with it specialized marketing, but the term only vaguely indicates the wide-flung areas into which technology has penetrated. Individual circumstances, personal inclinations, and opportunities must dictate the rep's choice.

For purposes of discussion here, it will simplify matters to broadly distinguish between the so-called "distributor" and "industrial" trades, recognizing that some firms are active in both but that most reps concentrate on one segment of the two divisions. Like kissin' cousins, they are related but differences between them can be profound. Basically, when you call on a distributor (be he wholesaler or retailer), you are dealing with a *merchant*. All he wants to know is, can he resell your whatchamatronics at a *profit*. In the other case, whatever may be the title of the man on whom you are calling, whether engineering buyer or what have you, the *usefulness* of your products is the primary issue.

The obvious, big advantage of being a "distributor rep" is that having sold him your line, it isn't a one-shot deal, as may be the case when selling industrials. Once you are "in," you have only to service the line, to pick up repeat orders. But another difference in approach to selling these two divisions deserves consideration: the personality of the rep calling on distributors looms up as of greater force than is the case with the man calling on industrial trade.

It is well that the distributor rep be a "good mixer."

Socializing with the owners and key employees can be of significant influence in selling the distributor trade. Your contacts there are likely to be the owners themselves or, if not that, the executive class of employees. "Ex post officio," these men can take the time, if so minded, to get away from business matters, verbally and physically. They are amenable to invitations for golfing, for an evening out on the town with your respective wives, for slipping out to have a sociable drink.

Of course there are all kinds of exceptions, as there must be in any generalization, but my point is that if you are gregarious, enjoy being with people, better opportunities for establishing intimate friendships are prevalent in dealing with distributors than with industrials. I guess I don't have to tell you the influence friendships have in determining whose line the distributor takes on.

By contrast, in calling on the industrials, ordinarily you meet only employees, usually far removed from "management." These men have sharply defined duties. Their time is curtailed and devoted, in the main, strictly to their jobs. Neither the opportunity nor the need occurs for turning business visits into social events beyond, perhaps an occasional luncheon date.

Selling to the industrial trade is an orderly, "in plant" process. For lack of better word, let's say it's more businesslike – perhaps I should say, formal. You deal systematically with individuals positioned for selecting and purchasing specific products and then having done with it. Ordinarily, you don't have to hang around, as in the case of trying to get the distributor's attention while he waits on customers, gets into prolonged phone conversations, discusses in-house problems with countermen while you stand around, swallowing your spit. Your time in talking with the industrial's engineer or buyer is limited to the matter in point. A call on a distributor can kill off the better part of a day, whereas you can make four or five calls on the industrials in the same period of time.

Repping is a highly personalized business – by its very nature, a fertile field for individualism, for men who think and do things "different." An outstanding example: recently, I saw a picture of a yacht that must have cost in the hundreds of thousands. It is owned by a man who "made it" as a rep. Back in the 1950's, he had just a pretty good size business, selling largely to distributors, his staff aggregating about a dozen people. To the amazement of his contemporaries suddenly, in one swoop, he deliberately gave up all his component lines, most of them nationally famous, to change his entire operation, to restrict himself thereafter solely to the sale of instruments and systems to end users.

In the 1960's, he retired – literally, a millionaire!

In so highly complex a section of industry as technology, the choice of which division to work in is entirely up to you. Make your decision and dig in; the addition of prayer should not be overlooked in helping determine that it be the right one.

6
THE ENGINEER AS A SALESMAN

– and vice versa

Now here is a subject on which the distinctions become quite fine. It resolves itself down to the dual question: can an engineer sell and do you have to be an engineer to sell technological products?

Traditionally, it has been said the highly skilled technician, i.e., the engineer, doesn't make a good salesman. With his habitual absorption in terms of design, production and usage of his device, it was assumed he would become so completely involved in the technical aspects of the products that he would lose sight of the fact he was supposed to be selling it. The old expression had it: the engineer would rather win the argument than make the sale.

Well, it goes without saying that the complexity of today's technology in many cases carries with it unquestionably the need for sales people to be capable of intelligently talking the language of the engineer. But how much of a technician do you have to be to sell the cabinet for housing a computer?

The more you know about what you are selling, the better, of course. That's axiomatic, from the very first page of the salesman's textbook. And true it is that in the electronic rep's conversation with a customer, technology is the basic language in which the discourse is held. But let's not get carried away, whatever your kind of "tronics" might be.

Among the limitless variety of products broadly included under the word "industry," are endless opportunities for sales people with little more than a modicum of technical expertise. Despite the overwhelming implications of such profound developments as "automation systems" and the like, some of the most desirable lines require only understanding of fundamentals, providing the other qualifications required for manufacturers' representation are present. To sell real estate successfully doesn't necessarily involve being an architect.

Let us not be stupidly disdainful of the intricate nature of what the technical rep has to sell but, it must be remembered, when the chips are down, the *technique of selling* can far offset requirements for understanding the technology involved.

I am quite sure that in some quarters, the inferences that extensive technical expertise need not always be paramount among a rep's qualifications will be roundly criticized. Buyers have been known to speak with good cause in disdainful terms of reps who "don't know their subject." It is a debatable point – one can only submit that circumstances alter cases. The business world has seldom evolved such an aptly descriptive term as, "the sales engineer." Fortunate indeed is the man capable of measuring up substantially to both parts of that title. In the final analysis, however, to place stress upon the one half or the other, depends on factors which are only within the individual rep's own circumstances, choice or ken.

7
APPLYING FOR A LINE

No time to be bashful

In one way or another, a rep has heard of a certain line available. He wants it. What does he do?

First, let me dispose of one minor but undesirable way of going after a line. I refer to that self-defeatist who describes himself as a "hungry" rep. Even for the beginner, it is ill-advised. It is intended to be persuasive assurance that he will work extra hard for a prospective principal. In actual fact, it indicates the very antithesis of the professional salesman – patently self-degrading, a revelation of incompetence, an admittance of failure. Its derogatory, begging implications are scarcely inducive to inspiring confidence when the sales manager is contemplating the kind of man who wants to represent his company. (However, there is no reason why one shouldn't point up having only a small number of lines, with consequently time to work on "just one more line." That's entirely different.)

As for the sales manager who blatantly proclaims he wants reps who are "hungry," he's of the same piece. It only means he has a dog line for which he can't get responsible, self-respecting men, so he looks for impoverished suckers, presumably willing to knock themselves out for a few crusts of his bread.

By the same token, the other extreme is just about as bad. Sometimes giving the appearance of great affluence can be enough in itself to kill your chances for picking up a good line. With due allowance for certain exceptions, sales managers are apt to shy away from what they call the "rich rep." They feel dubious about how hard such a rep will work the line if he doesn't have to. They don't welcome the idea of a rep whose financial independence makes him difficult to control, who's in a position to dispute, to tell the sales manager off if he so pleases.

It's the same old story – the happy medium is usually the best compromise.

Okay – so you've learned of a good line open that you'd sure like to have. The first order of things is to call the sales manager on the phone, of course. That's a must. It starts him right out with a favorable impression of your interest in his line, of your fast, aggressive way of doing business, that you're right on the ball. Plus, you can both feel each other out so much better verbally, than in writing. If the line is worth having at all, it's certainly worth the few dollars a phone call costs. But, regardless of whether a phonecon is held or not, a letter outlining your qualifications will be called for. What do you include in it?

Before answering that, let's consider the other side of the coin a minute. Reps frequently receive brief letters from manufacturers, stating little more than that they need a rep to sell such-and-such a line but, in return, they make preemptory demands for the rep's story of his life, or some facsimile thereof. The letter gives little to go by. There are innumerable manufacturers seeking reps, of whom too many are not worth the time of a busy rep to investigate. So, unless the manufacturer's name is immediately recognized and outstanding, such briefly worded letters are tossed away.

It works the same way in reverse. Consider how the sales manager regards an application for his line offering only meager information. Unless you've given him a convincing, full picture, your letter is likely to wind up in the round file. Use concise language but tell him plenty right in the beginning. Why not? What's to be bashful? Don't worry – he'll read it. Reps sometimes overlook the fact that the sales manager is just as anxious to secure the services of a good rep as you are to pick up a good line.

If you previously talked with him on the phone, repeat the salient points. He's probably conversed with several applicants and, not knowing them, might confuse you with another. When you list your firm's personnel, don't just stop at the number. Describe the key members' qualifications, starting with your own – degrees or other advanced education and experience, special abilities, years in service as well, of course, as how many years you have been in business.

Describe the territory you cover geographically. Name at least some of your best known lines or enclose your printed roster of lines. Include examples of your mailers, by way of demonstrating how you supplement personal calls with extra-curricular means of soliciting business. If you had some record-breaking experience, an outstanding increase in business, perhaps were awarded a distinction plaque, point that up.

Be sure to give the company names of well known people who are your customers. You'd think this superfluous, wouldn't you? It stands to reason that if you're covering a territory you would certainly be calling on the important accounts therein. Nevertheless, somehow it carries weight when you list familiarly the names of major customers. If you feel confident of the response, name individuals among them whom you suggest can be approached for reference purposes. (If you're sure of yourself this, too, can count heavily in your favor. The individual you name will probably feel flattered that you thought highly enough of him to offer his name for reference and will give you a big sendoff.)

List the trade organizations of which you are a member – such associations as MANA, ERA and IEEE, and of course Chamber of Commerce and similar respected organizations. Name your bank (why a sales manager needs to know this, I don't know, but it always seems to be impressive. Maybe it proves you are not a fly-by-night – you're responsible enough to have a bank account!)

And finally, if it's really an important line, don't lose time writing letters. Arrange an appointment, throw data on the pertinent things indicated into a briefcase and hop a first plane out for the manufacturer's city. Nothing, but nothing, beats face-to-face negotiation . . . . In any event, well, console yourself – it's a write-off if you don't get it. If you can't win 'em all, remember you don't win any if you don't try your damnedest in the first place!

8
THE SALES BOOK

– your showcase

If lines are your "stock in trade," the catalog sales book you carry with you on calls is a showcase.

It should look impressive, even opulant – orderly, neat, clean, especially *not* the dime store variety of binder. Why stress this? Because in indirect ways, you transmit to the prospect indications of how much *you* respect your lines. Presumably, you are the expert on them. By sloppiness with the literature, you deprecate it, perhaps even convey inferences of disdain for its contents. On the other hand, when you handle your literature as though you know it is important, that it deals with something of value, a similar assumption is subtly created in the prospect's mind. (The same reasoning holds true when presenting a sample. Don't just toss it out carelessly or superciliously. Lay it out with even exaggerated but evident care, indicating that *you*, knowing what it is, have *respect* for the little jewel .... It's an attitude that becomes contagious.)

There are many forms of binders for a salesman's catalog book – some quite ingenious but tricky when it comes to conveniently and quickly inserting or removing a catalog. Experience proves that nothing will serve better than a sturdy, top-quality, three-ring, looseleaf binder, providing it has *plenty of capacity* for easy readability while lying open on the desk or in your lap.

(And watch yourself when you lay your book out on the buyer's desk. Some guys take a dim view of scratches in their highly polished desk tops, nor do they take kindly to having their paper piles shoved around.)

Organize that salesbook – not only alphabetically but use an indexed divider for each section, i.e., with a tab label for each division of the line, such as catalogs and general product descriptions, pictures, technical data, drawings, testimonial letters or QPL's, advertising reprints, data on competitors and so on, so that you can flip quickly to any portion you want to discuss. (Note that I didn't include "price sheets" among the foregoing divisions. Not that you shouldn't carry these with you, but position them after everything else. Price is the *last* thing a good salesman wants to talk about!)

It's a comforting, confidence-inspiring feeling to have with you a *complete*, well-arranged salesbook when making your calls. Always carry it with you so that almost every question can be answered right on the spot. Don't make it necessary to apologize for the necessary data being "back at the office" or "out in your car" when, as the moment for the kill approaches, you have the prospect's keen interest aroused.

The time and few dollars expended on a *good* salesbook is well rewarded.

9
BOUND CATALOGS FOR CUSTOMERS

Forget it! Line card ideas

Sooner or later you will be confronted with the presumed need of compiling complete files of your catalogs to distribute among customers. You'll consider assembling them in attractive, expensive binders, with indexes, with each catalog tabbed, and so on – representing very substantial costs per each "book" and the expenditure of lots of time putting them together. I don't suppose there are many experienced reps who haven't gone down this long, costly road.

The situations where these objects of art pay off are few and far between. The buyer to whom you hand your brainchild will say Thanks, he'll murmur complimentary remarks while flipping through it, then place the book on a shelf somewhere and, in most cases, will very likely forget it. At some future time you'll find him requesting a catalog on some particular line, whereas he has it right there, in that binder! Grrh!

Take the case of the extensive catalog library maintained by some of the larger organizations. They'll disassemble your compilation, discard the binder, and file the catalogs according to their own idea of headings.

Again: the catalogs are soon out of date, this business being what it is, or factories issue supplements from time to time. Knowing the customer won't do it, *you* start with the firm intention of keeping your binders updated for the customer. But, I guarantee – you won't keep it up!

Sure, I'm a cynic when it comes to these elaborate, costly catalog file jobs bound for customers! Ask *any* old-time rep what *he* thinks of how wasteful these things can be! See if he doesn't pronounce them an exercise in futility. There may be a few, but very few, places where these productions are worth what they cost.

Now, *line cards* – that's different. A well laid out, comprehensive finger-tip listing of your line roster, with the concise, basic information a buyer needs, *that* he'll welcome and keep on tap – in fact, he expects you to supply such a list.

Line rosters can be knocked out cheaply – on ordinary stationary or, much better, printed on light card stock (known to the printers as "index"). The latter is preferable for impressiveness, easy to locate when needed and for ability to withstand hard usage. Convenient, standard three-hole punching adds the assurance that the buyer will insert it in his own desk binder – immediately, before it becomes misplaced.

Outside of logos and perhaps a short slogan, don't clutter it up with blurb stuff. Give the buyer only the data he needs for quick reference. But don't underdo it. Some reps list only the names of their lines, overlooking the fact that, with hundreds of such names crossing his desk, it's hard for the buyer to know just which one has identifying meaning for him (especially since so many manufacturers have such closely similar names). An important adjunct to such identification is a thumbnail description of the products under the manufacturer's name. You might show whether or not local stocks are available.

Keep the card simple in composition, and don't print too many at a time. Plan on reprinting and distributing them at least twice a year. Date it; use a different color stock for distinguishing purposes each time you put out replacement copies.

A different idea for a line roster handout is a kind of

deluxe elaboration of the usual line card. Like this:

Use a standard file folder, preferably of some distinctive color. Have your name, address and phone number (the last item big) imprinted across the tab. On the inner left side of the folder, name your lines, with a thumbnail product description under each.

On the inside right hand cover, under the heading "Ordering Information," list the names of your lines but follow each one with terms and F.O.B. point, plus freight allowances, with perhaps a notation concerning local stock availability. If you don't care to show pricing, note on the bottom that because it is confidential information, writing in the discount structure, quantity price breaks and so on, are left to the buyer's own judgment.

Spaces will show up useful for printing your phone number prominently; you may want to insert a slogan, perhaps some brief wording about your fine-and-dandy service, etc. Have it standard three-hole punched for the customer who prefers things like this in his binder rather than in a drawer file.

Aside from the self-evident value of this data folder to the buyer, it provides an impressive way to enclose a quotation, some important letter or a new price list etc. when you are hand-delivering such an item. Subsequent items pertaining to your lines can be conveniently filed in the same folder.

Such a line-folder can be produced quite inexpensively. Folders are standard stationery items. Type the copy and have it reproduced by offset printing. That's about all there is to it, but this makes an impressive promotional piece, one which your customer will be glad to hang on to.

10
THE SECOND OFFICE

'Bye, dear – I'll try to get home early.

You've moved your business out of your first "office," i.e., your home where (like so many of us) you started. You figured with pencil and paper very critically just how much business you must bring in to pay the rent of the new office. You selected a spot strategically located with respect to fast access to and from customers and the corresponding cost of gasoline. You've avoided getting hooked into paying electrical space heating bills because they can kill yuh. You took cognizance of the fact that the rent undertaken should be modest, based on an office being a workshop – not necessarily a show room. In short, you've got a good sense of economics and you're going to go places!

Before getting on to more important subjects, a word or two about the basic equipment: if you're buying a typewriter, I hope you pass up those with the elite type – too small and looks affected for business correspondence. Likewise, that you're not getting fancy type like imitation script or other distracting departures from standard styles – freakishness, ostentation, don't do your image any good. The easier it is to read your letter, the more likely it is to be read! At least two keys (you may want more) not ordinarily supplied on the usual keyboard are desirable, such as a one-key "plus-minus" symbol and one that imprints the small "o" as a degrees symbol, used so often in technical correspondence.

A commodious catalog rack, alphabetically arranged, is a must. The standardized metal contraptions available seldom fit well within a given space; the shelving dimensions waste space when employed for catalogs which are usually somewhere around 8½" x 11". Have a wooden rack built (could be an easy do-it-yourself job). Use two fairly thick end panels for each section. The kind the supply houses sell for making steps are perfect. Dado them, with the grooves at about 3" intervals, so that you can expand or contract the shelves according to the height of each catalog stack. Use ¼" fiberboard for the shelves, shaped to slip easily in and out of the grooves. Outer dimensions, bracing, and number of sections are up to your judgment in completing this simple carpentering job.

Just one hint – you *never* have enough catalog storage space. Anticipate! Plan right from the start for additional space which *will* be required, I guarantee!

Just as soon as you can afford it, get yourself a copier. It's one of the most useful adjuncts you can possibly have in the way of office equipment. There are excellent makes now available for two or three hundred dollars. In time alone, they'll save that for you again and again.

But, fixing up an office adequately is no big deal. Let's move on to something much more critical, complex and mandatory for conducting a business properly – such as comprehensive, time-saving, economical office records. You might say, records form the skeleton supporting your business structure, so let's get down to the bare bones of the subject. (Joke).

11
ROUTINE FORMS AND GOLD

Who needs electronic data processing?

Keeping written track of what goes on in a rep business has produced a dubious variety of office routine record forms. Some of these no doubt are excellent in providing for the entries required, others adequate and there are those which would be more useful for wrapping fish.

Be that as it may, every rep business should have a minimum of *three basic forms* – comprehensive, supplying the vital data needed for the operation of a properly administered business. These sheets need not be cumbersome, complex in layout or laborious to use; the costs can be nominal in time, effort and money, and still do the job effectively.

I also submit that three *properly* designed record forms are the most required for up to a several-man organization. Anything more than that begins to approach the law of diminishing returns – until, that is, you get to the state of requiring EDP.

Everyone is familiar with the indubitable value of electronic data processing. Many reps sell EDP components or systems. Yet it is notable that not too many rep firms use EDP themselves in the operation of their own offices, mainly because of the time required to compile the data for feeding into the computer and costs of the processing. But to conduct a business intelligently, good routine records are absolutely essential and this can be readily accomplished without resorting to the elaborations of EDP.

The three referenced basic forms should supply the following information:

1. *Order history*: a completely detailed set of data, recording every step of each order's progress, from the moment you take the order until you receive the commission for it.
2. *Sales Volume Record*: in dollars, for a current month or for any selected period, for each of your lines.
3. *Salesman's Call Record*: recaps of individual salesman's calls.

Let's start with the *Order Record* (see facsimile, end of chapter). Varying conditions in your activities may call for some minor differences but, otherwise, this form will provide all the information you should have governing the processing and history of each order.

Make these up on any ordinary 8½ x 11 stationery – no need to be fancy. Three-hole punch each sheet for fastening into a binder.

Note the form is divided into two sections. Up to the double perpendicular is the data *you* supply. After that follows the conclusive information which can come only from the factory.

Value of two order dates: you have the evidence right there if, as and when the expediter throws at you the date appearing on the order rather than when you actually received it (which might be much later).
The buyer's name: useful to jog your memory if any future discussion arises concerning the order.
Description: You can use this in several ways.
1) The most simple, if you don't write too many orders within a particular period, is to enter here (by abbreviations) the customer's name, the brand and catalog number of the item(s). This is quick and concise. For the smaller operations or for reps who handle mainly (and not too plentiful!) big ticket items, this is entirely adequate.
2) By principal: set up separate sheets for each principal. In this case, you enter only the customer's name and item(s)

under "Description." Note that it enables you to quickly determine the activity on each line, aside from providing detailed order history. Generally speaking, it is the best way to use this column.

An addition to the foregoing would be to set up separate sheets for *individual customers.* Under "Description" you would then enter only the manufacturer's name and item(s) catalog number. By this duplication of the form, you have a complete record of how much business you are getting from selected customers. It's not likely that you would want or need this for *every* customer but you might have reason in certain cases. Examples: you may have a customer who places orders very frequently for one particular line; it would be convenient to set up a sheet separately just for this customer and principal. It could be revealing by way of proving whether or not some particular customer is worth all the service he requires. If it is your policy to divide accounts by salesmen, this would provide a precise record of the referenced accounts' business for crediting the salesmen accordingly. Other purposes for keeping this order history specifically by customer will occur to you.

Delivery dates: it is particularly worthwhile to have before you differences between the "Del. Req." which stands for date *requested* by the customer and the factory's *acknowledgement* date which specifies the actual promised date. For example: the expediter, when complaining about delivery, will invariably cite the date *requested* when the order was placed.

Invoice data: your final evidence that the order has been completed and shipped.

Commission: when commission is received, enter date and amount or, if you prefer, just enter date and check mark. Aside from the obvious, it is not at all infrequent that a principal's bookkeeping department misses paying you for an order. It can and does happen!

Glancing over the form facsimile should make its value self-evident. A few moments each day filling in these simple entries enables you to follow the progress of each order step by step and gives you a complete history for future reference. There will be many times, I warrant you, when you will be mighty glad you had it all there, at your finger tips.

Next, the *sales volume record*. Keep it simple! All you want here is dollar figures. Set up a sheet for each of your factories. *Every day* enter on one line the date, the customer's name and p.o. number and the total *dollars* amount of each order as you receive it – nothing else is necessary (or desirable in this case). What does this do for you?

Instead of guesstimating, at any time you can tell precisely how much business you are doing during the current month, instead of depending on the vagaries of memory or having to wade through stacks of perhaps applicable but miscellaneous pieces of paper. You can check progress or lack of it from month to month. You can readily make comparisons with sales volume for any given period in previous years. It provides a concrete base from which to make sales forecasts for any one or all of your lines. Not the least is that you have actual figures at your fingertips to confound the sales manager who exaggerates in his complaints about how little you are doing for him. And, these figures are also useful as another check against commission statements.

Finally, the record of the *salesman's calls* (see facsimile, end of chapter). This simple sheet ought to be printed on gold, it is that valuable.

Because the nature of the information required to record is self-evident, I have indicated just about only the important entries to be made. Make this form up yourself as you see it BUT *keep it simple*! Believe me – if it calls for a lot of entries, your man (or you) just won't keep it up. If you complicate it, you will defeat its purpose. In its comparative informality lies its worth. (I just can't stress this too much – people are so apt to get "form happy," not knowing where to stop – and consequently reach the point of no return. KEEP IT SIMPLE!)

Use the form when you are planning your day's calling agenda, by inserting the name, address, etc. of each call on separate sheets *before* you leave the office, arranging them according to the call location. (On the *back* of each sheet, jot down the subjects you intend to discuss.)

Interviews with prospective customers can be lengthy. Many facts are brought out which have bearing on the future. We are all prone to depending on memory for the follow-up call. That's a mistake. The life of a rep is too busy, too full, to rely on memory for what happened on the occasion of each call.

It is most important that the essential facts be recorded on this form while fresh in the salesman's mind. Set the example yourself and enforce it with your men. As you leave the prospect's premises, you get into your car. Take a couple of minutes right then and there, before you turn the switch on, to note briefly the results of your call: the requests for catalogs, samples or quotes, the buyer's promise to let you know, the names of other individuals having influence there, the possibility of buying at some future time, the price he claims competition is offering, the items in which he showed pronounced interest, some peculiarity of what he likes or doesn't, date for the next call, etc.

Keep this record on file, positioned chronologically to be at hand for your follow-up call on the same customer. Fasten the results of the second call to the first sheet. Continue the same process with each succeeding call. You will have thereby accumulated a record of priceless information leading to finally getting the order.

Sometimes you work up a deal, only to be told that

action on it has been postponed to some time in the future. Months later, the deal comes to life. What a blessing it can be to have all the pertinent data available for refreshing yourself on the details all in one package! Or, after it has become dim in your memory, it serves as a reminder when the time comes for following up. (It is not out of the way to note that some 80% of business garnered takes an average of five contacts for consumation.) The file can also serve for purposes of written reference when your factory man calls and you are discussing what happened or is to be expected in the case of some particular deal.

One way of handling these files (or packages) is to arrange them in folders that are date tabbed, in sequence setting up your calling days' agendas. As each date comes up, you can select from that folder the packages for calls on customers who are geographically adjacent. Of course, a prospect's file may indicate you were to call on him on a day that turns out to be one in which you are too embroiled in other matters to make it. In that event, you simply move the package ahead to the next possible date.

I make a point of what should be obvious because the hazard in this system is becoming enslaved to it. I certainly do not mean it at all derogatory when I say the rep is, by nature of his calling, an opportunist. *First things come first.* On the date you intended to follow up on a prospective deal, you get an urgent call from an important customer who wants to see you right away. His premises are in an entirely different location from the direction of the previously intended call. Every bit of judgment should be brought to bear in determining which way you go. Despite the *prospective* deal, remember that a customer on the books is worth two in the bushes.

But getting back to the call record itself, repeat: make your notes as soon as you leave the customer's place. Don't wait until you get back to the office. You're human, man!

You'll forget! You'll come back to the office to find that something distracting has happened, to absorb all your attention. You'll postpone making the record of that call; some of the data will fade from your memory.

An alternative to the paper form, as used by some reps, is to carry a dictating machine on calls. The data is voice recorded, to be repeated again by transcribing later in the office, which now ties in the time of your secretary. This is certainly better than nothing but in effect it involves recording the same data twice; otherwise, how are you going to build up a file recording your successive calls? And, they cost money.

Many firms use cards, usually in the neighborhood of 3" by 5", as records of sales calls. These don't begin to approach the value of full 8½ x 11 sheets. There isn't room to make extended entries. You can't fasten them together for filing purposes. They are easily misplaced. Cards aren't much better than a pocket notebook or the back of an old envelope!

You can add to and multiply record forms endlessly. You can have a form for analyzing costs per call, another for keeping track of the number of calls you make per account as contrasted to the amount of business forthcoming. You can make up a form that will show up the costs of handling one line as compared to another, while contrasting the amounts of commission each provides.

It can go on and on. Multiplying your golden piles of paper can turn them into dross; you and your staff can become so immersed in paper work that you won't have time to get out and pick up the orders which supply the data needed to build up those piles.

In short: if you feel you need more information than that provided by those three basic forms, you are ready for electronic data processing.

PURCHASE ORDER RECORD

Date	P.O. number	Qnty	Description	$ each	Del. req'td	Akngmt date	INVOICE date	INVOICE number	INVOICE amount	COMM.

Enter 2 dates – one, the date order actually received. The other, the date written on the customer's order. Indicate "received" by "R" preceding date.

Helpful to insert name or nickname of buyer below number

See text

Delivery requested = NOT the promised date

Factory's actual promised date

SALESMAN'S CALL RECORD

Called__________

ompany____________________ Follow-up__________

ddress____________________

hone ____________________

ndividuals to see: Position: Bldg./phone ext.

ee next time:

esults:

Brands or items discussed

Favorable Or?

Reactions of individuals seen

Literature left Quotes

Requests for quotes or other info

To remember for next call

etc.

etc.

etc.

Salesman__________

12
THE REP AS A CREDITOR

Low man on the totem pole

It's all very well to have faith – but when you contemplate someone is going to owe you money, it makes sense to determine beforehand whether or not the assets are there to pay you. So many reps have been stung by manufacturers who, for one reason or another, failed to meet their obligations when the chips were down! In many cases it was a lack of foresight on the rep's part that caused his loss.

A rep may look with doubt at a fifty-dollar check tendered by a stranger and will demand satisfactory identification before he accepts it. Yet, that same rep may take on a new line, on which he will risk hundreds to thousands of dollars out of his own pocket, while making no very real effort to be assured of the principal's financial responsibility – this, in the face of the fact that as many as 10,000 cases of business failures have been reported in a year.

Sometimes the rep has secured the all-important financial statements, has consulted the principal's ratings in national credit agencies, has checked with banks, with his trade associations, with other reps who may know the manufacturer – in short, he has taken every possible step to assure himself that the manufacturer is in good financial shape. That kind of rep will do all right. In most cases, he will have no problems on that score.

But, let's assume that for a period all goes well; and, tempus fugit. A manufacturer falls upon bad times. Maybe production difficulties, credit losses, embezzlement, tough competition or what have you, makes him a bankrupt. It can and has happened, many times. Among his obligations are commissions due to the representatives. What chance does the rep stand for collection?

Of course, if the assets are small and the obligations large, he might as well charge it up to experience and hope for better luck next time. But suppose the bankrupt is able to pay off a goodly or substantial part of his debts. What is the rep's position in order of creditors to be paid? Up to this writing, he comes pretty close to being low man on the totem pole.

Some years ago, while a member of ERA's Government Affairs Committee, I dug into this sad state of affairs. After considerable exploration, I received a final answer from my then Congressman, a letter which read in part:

> "After writing to you yesterday, I talked with Mr. Ernest Giesling of the Administration Office of the United States Courts and he read me Section 64-a-2 of the Bankruptcy Code and that section specifically classifies those working on commission with the regular salaried employees so far as priority of their claims in case of bankruptcy *provided the commissions have been earned within three months prior to the filing of the bankruptcy and do not exceed $600.00."*

Not very helpful, eh? It is not uncommon for perfectly sound principals to owe reps commission for more than three months, for one reason or another. And a shaky manufacturer can easily stall his reps along, far beyond three months.

As for the $600 limitation: reps have principals many states away. Who is going to undertake long distance legalities for so small an amount? Figure costs of time consumed, the attorney's or collection agency's cut; what would be left for the rep where the amount is under $600.00?

There is, however, some hope. While preparing the material for this book, I re-checked again, this time with my current Congressman, and was told by his office that the situation has not changed but that "the Congress recently authorized a commission to study the existing bankruptcy laws of the United States and to recommend changes." That development was then expedited when Congress specified a two-year period to delve broadly into bankruptcy, its causes and philosophy, with the hope that the Commission would come up with improvements in the Bankruptcy Act. President Nixon appointed three members to this body: Harold Marsh, Jr., a well-known attorney; Wilson Newman, a top official with Dun and Bradstreet and Charles Seligson, a New York University law professor. In addition, Chief Justice Burger was to appoint three more members. The Commission also included four members from the Congress: Rep, Wiggins (Calif.), Sen. Burdick (N.D.), Sen. Cook (Ky.), and Rep. Byron G. Rogers (Colo.).

It would be well for every rep to take it upon himself to contact his Congressman and, if possible, others of the Commission, urging that provisions be made *to accord creditor status equal to that of the bankrupt's employees.* You might also stress two points; that to arbitrarily impose a limitation on legitimate amounts claimed is unreasonable and that there should be no time limitation on the obligation incurred shorter than at least a year preceding the bankruptcy proceedings.

Why should you bother? Because, my friend, if you stay in business long enough, *you* are going to be confronted some day with this situation. The inexorable laws of economics make it inevitable.

In the meantime, the course should be clear: if it's a new principal, "investigate before you invest." In the case of the established principal, for more reasons than the obvious one, keep a sharp eye on the *dates* on which you receive commission checks. Some manufacturers mail out their checks always on or about the same day. Others are variable, but normally stay within reasonable relationship to an established date. In the course of time, a pattern develops.

The moment some serious irregularity in that pattern occurs, you will do well to sit up and take notice! It's easiest for a manufacturer having financial difficulties to slight his reps, rather than other creditors. He can usually count on the rep's diffidence, on fear of offending his principals. Before long, the manufacturer might be owing the rep a lot of money. If his problems become serious, the rep is in trouble.

Undue delays in commission payments are glibly explained in various ways. "We've switched bookkeepers and the new guy hasn't got with it yet." "We're changing our accounting to a computerized system – we're in a temporary state of confusion." "The man who signs checks has been delayed coming back from Europe." "Your check went out. Must have been lost in the mails." "The record of your commissions got mixed up with another territory – we're trying to straighten it out."

Delays in forwarding your check may be due entirely to legitimate, exceptional incidents, to unlooked-for breaks in regular routine, not at all necessarily related to lack of funds, and soon to be corrected. "Soon," that is! Because if not "soon," you'd better start demanding something more negotiable than explanations before you are assigned to that low-down position on the totem pole.

13
TRADE ASSOCIATIONS

Antithesis of the lone wolf

A commonplace feature of the American business world is the trade association. From the very roots of our country's formation, the principles of strength in union has always been a basic part of our existence. It applies no less to manufacturers' representation.

Of course, trade associations can vary from loosely organized, weakly supported groups out to the few vigorous, highly active associations. As may be noted, the Electronic Representative Association is referenced at several points in this book, by way of exemplifying the workings of an efficient grouping of professional firms. No better illustration serves of how valuable an effective, cooperative organization can be for its members and the trade, than that of ERA. Those involved in technological sales but not entirely familiar with this association's operations, may find the following brief description of pertinent interest:

The Electronic Representatives Association is an important, influential factor in today's relationship with the electronic trade. It is a distinctive, highly regarded organization, the modern day outgrowth of a succession of groups formed from the very beginning of the electronic industry. It has reached high levels as a result of innumerable men giving freely of time and effort in association, aware that by helping the other fellow, one helps oneself.

Today, ERA is composed of more than 1,700 member firms and branches across the country. Its roster grows continually as newcomers become aware of the membership benefits available. It has earned the respect of industry as an association of responsible firms, joined in common cause, devoted to constantly elevating standards and conditions of the professional independent salesman.

Through many years as a member, this writer has had the privilege of serving in various official capacities with ERA, at one time known as "The Representatives of Electronic Products Manufacturers, Inc.".* As a result of being closely identified with the manner of its workings, I can testify to the advantages of membership in such an association as ERA. They range from the very specific through the intangible.

There is the prestige, the professional status accorded the ERA image. Members are entitled to attend ERA's basic and advanced management institutes conducted at leading universities, to take part in edifying workshops at trade shows. Economical group insurance rates, in all common categories, are available. Lists of lines offered for representation are issued periodically. Members are publicized in national and local chapter directories. At meetings, members "break bread" with fellow reps, developing friendships in place of cut-throat competition. Valuable information is exchanged; meeting programs include interesting speakers, instructive films . . .

Note that ERA is selected as an example only to portray an association concentrating specifically on one industry. There are those which cover broad spectrums; as an illustration, the highly regarded "Manufacturers' Agents National Association" includes several thousand firms of representatives

*One small but perpetuating contribution of which the writer is never through bragging is that, back in 1958, in an inspired moment of exasperation as he stumbled over the organization's lengthy, cumbersome name, he authored the name by which the Association has since been known.

and agents engaged in just about every industry imaginable. MANA is active in public relations, legislative affairs, holds regional seminars in cooperation with educational institutions, offers excellent insurance programs, group discounts for its members, publishes the monthly, edifying "Agency Sales Magazine" and, in general includes a host of membership benefits impractical to detail here. It should be considered, too, that reps can find good reason to be members of an association (or "society") specializing in one field along with holding membership in an all embracing organization such as MANA.

Nowadays, we hear much of the need for becoming "involved", of joining in common causes intended to bring about some aspect of better conditions for mankind; at the same time, one need not feel at all selfish in paying particular heed to the pragmatic advantages of helping further the interests of the industry in which one has to make a living. Incidentally, not the least of such "advantages" is the frequently occuring enlightenment that, by contact in person with a competitor in a mutual cause, you learn, as a matter of fact, that the other fellow isn't at all the S.O.B. he was made out to be, that he can turn out to be just a real nice guy, like yourself earnestly and legitimately trying to make a decent buck or two.

"No man is an island – " To be independent does not alter the need for joining in with and cooperating with one's contemporaries. The complex inter-twining of modern-day business life makes an anachronism of the lone wolf operation. As human beings, in the interests of self-preservation and advancement, we need each other. For the rep to be a member of a recognized, legitimate trade association, taking full part in its activities, is a realization of his contribution to the common interests of all – his own, no less than that of his fellow men.

14
SALES AGREEMENTS

Guide lines and suggested provisions

Sales agreements between manufacturer and representative range from the deceptive simplicity of verbal "understandings" or perhaps a letter, all the way out to formidable, multi-page documents. (Some of these last named can be needlessly verbose, employing much obtuse legal jargon, best regarded by the thoughtful rep with a barrel-full of salty skepticism.)

Outside of the usual, two points should be particularly watched out for. One, your agreement should make unequivocally clear that product warranties, with performance expressed or implied, are solely the responsibility of the manufacturer. The other, a new kink some reprehensible character has introduced, is a real cutie. This is a manufacturers' inclusion of a provision by which the rep agrees he will not take on representation of a competitive or similar product line in the event of termination – like, perhaps, for two years thereafter! Needless to say, you should refuse to fetter the livelihood of your future with such a manifestly unfair prohibition.

Obvious enough, a contractual agreement is bad business if it isn't fair to both parties. If the rep is diffident about insisting on self-protective clauses, he is only inviting trouble for the future. One fact cannot be emphasized too many times: it is as important to the manufacturer that he have the services of a good rep, as it is for the rep to secure a good line; it's a two-way street. In any event, you might note that more and more, smart reps are consulting their attorneys before formalizing representation agreements. Most manufacturers do – shouldn't you, too?

The breadth and depth of experience which a good trade association can bring to bear on an industry-wide problem is well demonstrated in a most thoughtful, comprehensive report on the subject of sales agreements by a special Electronic Representatives Association committee. Though not intended to be all-conclusive, because every negotiation between a manufacturer and rep is special, the wide range of its provisions makes the report an excellent reference source for the setting up of a representation arrangement. As general guide lines for the main points to be covered, by ERA permission, gratefully acknowledged, a slightly condensed version is presented in the pages that follow.

SAMPLE CONTRACT

THIS AGREEMENT made this ......day of ....19 , by and between VIDEO HEALTH SYSTEMS, INC , a corporation under the laws of the State of PA , having its principal office at WAYNE PA , hereinafter referred to as "Manufacturer" and a corporation under the laws of the State of having its principal office at , hereinafter referred to as "Representative," as follows:

Manufacturer appoints Representative as its exclusive selling representative to sell products (enumerated below) in the territory (as defined below); and Representative accepts the appointment and agrees to sell and promote the sale of the Manufacturer's products.

Territory: Representative's territory shall consist of the following:

Products: The "products" of the manufacturer to be sold by the Representative are: VIDEOTAPE PROGRAMS OF AN EDUCATIONAL NATURE

Representative's compensation shall be ....% of the "net invoice price" of the Manufacturer's product shipped into Representative's territory. However, when engineering, execution of the order, or shipment involve different territories, the Manufacturer will split the full commission among the Representatives whose territories are involved. The Manufacturer will make this determination and advise the interested Representatives.

Commissions are due and payable on or before the .... day of the month following the month in which shipment is made . . . . At the time of payment, Manufacturer will send Representative a commission statement showing the computation of commissions and copies of the invoices covered by the commission statement.

"Net invoice price" shall mean the total price at which an order is invoiced to the customer, but excluding shipping and mailing costs, taxes, insurance and cash discounts granted to the customer by the Manufacturer.

There shall be deducted from any sums due Representative:

i) An amount equal to commissions previously paid or credited on sales of Manufacturer's products; which have since been returned by the customer or on allowances credited to the customer for any reason by the Manufacturer; and

ii) An amount equivalent to commissions previously paid or credited on sales which Manufacturer shall not have been fully paid by the customer whether by reason of the customer's bankruptcy, insolvency, or any other reason which, in Manufacturer's judgment, renders the account uncollectible.

(If any sums are ever realized upon such accounts, Manufacturer will pay Representative its percentage of commission applicable at the time of the original sale upon the net proceeds of such collection).

"Order" shall mean any commitment to purchase Manufacturer's products which calls for shipment into Representative's territory or which is subject to split commission in accordance with the provision pertaining thereto.

All orders are subject to acceptance or rejection by an authorized officer of Manufacturer. Manufacturer shall be responsible for all credit risks and collections.

If Manufacturer notifies customer of its acceptance or rejection of an order, a copy shall be transmitted to the Representative. At least once every month, Manufacturer shall supply Representative with copies of all orders received directly by Manufacturer, copies of all shipping notices or invoices originated at the time of shipment, and copies of all correspondence and quotations made to customers in the territory.

All sales shall be at prices and upon terms established by Manufacturer.

Representative shall use its best efforts and devote such time as may be reasonably necessary to sell and promote the sale of Manufacturer's products.

Representative will conduct all of its business in its own name and in such manner as it may see fit. Representative will pay all expenses whatever of its office and activities and be responsible for the acts and expenses of its employees.

Representative shall not, without prior written consent of Manufacturer, handle products which, in the opinion of Manufacturer are competitive with the products of the Manufacturer being handled by the Representative.

Nothing in this Agreement shall be construed to constitute the Representative as the partner, employee or agent of the Manufacturer nor shall either party have any authority to bind the other in any respect, it being intended that each shall remain an independent contractor responsible only for its own actions.

Manufacturer shall be solely responsible for the design, development, supply, production and performance of its products and the protection of its trademarks.

Manufacturer shall furnish Representative, at no expense to Representative, a reasonable quantity of samples, catalogs, literature and any other material necessary for the proper promotion and sale of its products in the territory.

Terms of Agreement and Termination. This Agreement shall be effective on the .... day of ....19 ...., and shall continue in force until terminated by either party at the end of any calendar month, by giving not less than .... days written notice to the other by registered or certified mail.

Rights Upon Termination. Upon termination of this Agreement for any reason, Representative shall be entitled to:

a) commissions on all orders calling for shipment into Representative's territory which are dated or communicated to Manufacturer prior to the effective date of termination; and

b) its share of split commission on orders dated or communicated to Manufacturer prior to the effective date of termination regardless of when such orders are shipped.

Disputes and Arbitration. The parties agree that any disputes or questions arising hereunder including the construction or application of this Agreement shall be settled by arbitration in accordance with the rules of the American Arbitration Association then in force.

IN WITNESS WHEREOF, the parties hereto have executed this Agreement the day and year first above written in multiple counterparts, each of which shall be considered an original.

MANUFACTURER:

By .... Title ....

REPRESENTATIVE:

By .... Title ....

Additional notes

Some manufacturers may wish to include a special provision pertaining to commissions on military or other government business.

The Agreement should cover all products and services of the Manufacturer, unless the Representative is to handle only specific products or services. It is preferable not to list products by model or part number as these may change from time to time.

The Agreement should also indicate whether or not the following are to be included:
(a) Order for engineering
(b) Research and development
(c) Non-recurring start-up costs
(d) Cancellation charges
(e) Tooling
(f) Environmental qualification and specification
(g) Compliance testing
(h) Drawings and handbooks
(i) Documentation
(j) Packaging
(k) Repair and reworks.

The Agreement should establish a program of "severance payments." For example: one month's severance pay for each 2 full years as the Representative of the Manufacturer, with a maximum number of months of severance pay which can be earned (i.e., 12 months). Each such payment shall be 1/12th of the total commissions payable to Representative in the 12 calendar months preceding the effective date of such termination.

15
TAKING DISTRIBUTOR INVENTORIES

Should one?

To the distributor rep, there is no chore quite so disagreeable as taking inventory of his line on the customers' shelves. Nor so rewarding!

The rep who climbs up and down shelves, counting the pieces, noting the items that need more frequent replenishing, the absence of numbers that the distributor ought to stock but doesn't, has only to wash up, sit down with the distributor and, forearmed with the applicable information, can almost invariably build up the order bigger than had it been left to the customer's own procedures.

It's as simple as that – a tedious, time-consuming job, but one that pays off. The rep who thinks that, as a professional salesman, such plebeian work is beneath his dignity, might make comparisons to the common practice of the lawyer who, in the course of preparing to appear in court, first arms himself thoroughly by researching the technical points bearing on his case – to him, likewise, a tedious, time-consuming job.

I had been telling the president of one of my factories about a minor incident concerned with taking a distributor's inventory. He mused,

"If all my reps inventoried distributors' stocks periodically, our business would be doubled. But," he shrugged pessimistically, "only five of them do."

"How do you know it's only five?" I queried curiously.

"Not only the sales volume itself. Some territories have

better potential than others. But I can see it in the orders. I watch for items being specified in increasing quantity, for products that had not been included previously, of the kind which had no special attractions other than being a regular item in the line. And on subsequent orders, I also follow up to see if newly added items are being re-ordered. To me, things like that mean the rep has been counting numbers. "Sure," he grinned, "it's not infallible, but a line like ours is pretty standard. Such increases are only accomplished by a rep who's on the ball; taking inventories himself means he's pushing and prodding the distributor into giving us bigger and better orders."

Well, for whatever it's worth, I leave you with that opinion, except to add the man I quoted is nationally known to be one of the country's most astute and successful manufacturers in his field. By the way, I have often quoted something else I once heard this same desk-pounding executive propounding at the top of his voice: "I tell my people to answer the rep's questions fast! I tell them to get those answers out on toilet paper, if they must – but get them out *fast*!" Despite the deplorable Rabelaisian choice of expression, one might wish all principals were as similarly cognizant of the urgent need for replying promptly to the reps' pleas for answers.

16
CONVENTIONS

and how to get lucky

IEEE, NEW, CES, WESCON, NEC, NEPCON – if the number of Shows continues to proliferate, we'll exhaust the alphabet as a means of identifying them! Upon the advent of a convention in some distant city, you'll probably also hear things like:

"There's too many Shows – they're just a lotta waste of time and money."

"Guess you gotta go to keep some guy from stealing your line, eh?"

"Shows ain't what they used to be – customers used to come with their order pads and you did business – but them days are gone forever."

And so the cynics drone on and on with their dolorous pronouncements.

There are just enough grains of truth in the deprecating opinions of the wiseacres to justify doubt about the value of these Shows in the mind of the newcomer. Conventions do cost money. They do consume valuable time. For the rep who attends only in compliance with a principal's mandate, who then leaves the enforced sales meeting to head for home, a convention can be a pretty expensive proposition. Whether or not being there proves to be profitable, devolves upon the individual rep himself – and luck (but of the latter, more later).

Not only for the established rep but for the newcomer especially, conventions are an absolute must. If nothing else, the very manufacturers who are seeking representation are there. You should be, too. As discussed in the chapter describing how to get lines, the convention is a fertile field for planting the seeds from which lines grow.

The spirit of conviviality prevailing creates an atmosphere conducive to making acquaintances and establishing friendships which, just in the cold-blooded sense of business advantage alone, can lead to becoming one of your greatest assets. As a couple of pragmatic possibilities: the rep from a distant territory with whom you strike up a friendship may remember you when a principal happens to mention the fact that representation is being sought in your territory. In a group at one of the ubiquitous snack bars, you may meet a sales manager who, someday needing a rep out your way, might recall that you made a favorable impression on him. Do you meet such influential people while staying at home?

Sales meetings with your principals are frequently held during convention time. Sure, you might find some acceptable excuse for not attending but, aside from the value of meeting your principals face to face, among those present are key factory personnel, the men who don't make field trips who, up to that point, consisted of little more than names for you. Upon meeting them in person, ensuing conversations and incidents help you appraise how influential they may or may not be in the furtherance of your work with a given factory. Other possibilities occur for forming or cementing factory relationships, than which there is nothing more important in the existence of the manufacturers' representative.

In innumerable ways, far beyond detailing here, conventions offer means for helping make your name familiar, to enhance that all-important "image." In addition to the always uppermost thinking about acquiring lines, the opportunities afforded by the exhibits for studying "developments in the art," for learning what competitors are featuring, for exchanging ideas and methods with reps from other territories, make of the convention a forum for broadening the mind difficult to achieve in any other way.

As a veteran of conventioneering, I can testify that inevitably, sooner or sometimes many months later, something came up that made me glad I had been there. Or it can happen right on the spot. I recall the last day of one convention where, in the stifling, one hundred degree heat, without air conditioning, I was drooping, all but exhausted from traversing the huge tent in which the convention was housed. It will soon be over, thank heavens, I was thinking.

I stopped to chat with a rep acquaintance doing "booth duty" for one of his principals, a nationally famous manufacturer. Near his chair, I noticed a display of home-made cards, showing devices quite out of place in the spectacular exhibit of the booth's sophisticated products.

"That?" he responded to my question. "There's a little machine shop here in town where they make those gadgets. They're sometimes used with our products. When one of my customers is looking for a source, I refer them to this shop. Just doing them and the customer a favor – like I'm displaying their card here for them."

I speculated that the interesting devices might hold opportunities for exploitation. He shrugged. "I've got all I can handle right now. But here's the owner's phone number, if you want to give him a ring."

Just to satisfy my conscience that I had left no stone unturned in the way of a possible opportunity, I followed through. To make a long story shorter, I got together with the head of the outfit, a man skilled in his trade but a novice in marketing. I saw possibilities for expanding his product's usage and responded to his eager desire for professional guidance. I took the line on for my territory, established reps for him across the country (with an override for me as "sales manager"!) and, for some years, until the old gent decided to retire, the deal provided me with a very neat income.

For luck to strike, you've got to be an *available* target – and that means being in the right place at the right time. Conventions are a pretty likely f'r instance!

17
AUTO STATUS

Cadillac? Volkswagen?

You may wonder what the class of car you drive has to do with marketing. Well, there are some points to be made. Suppose, as frequently happens, you are taking a buyer out to lunch. By virtue of choice or circumstances, you may be driving one of those swanky, high-priced cars (need I name it?) Your evidence of affluence will make an impression on him, that's for sure – but not necessarily the kind you would like.

In the first place, you invite his envy – and that doesn't help put him in the right frame of mind toward you that leads to orders. Secondly, you may bring out his humanitarian instincts. If *you* can afford such a fancy car, you must be making oodles of money. Perhaps he should be giving his business to some poor devil who needs it, rather than you, you plutocrat.

How about those occasions when you are chauffeuring a visiting sales manager around the territory? Suppose, as is likely, he drives only a middle-class car. Not only may you arouse *his* envy (which won't do you any good) but he may think you're making too much money and decide to cut your commission rate!

Now, one should be fair about this. Some reps will argue, with a certain amount of plausibility, that the more prosperous you appear to be, the more you must be selling. If your products are that popular, they must be good – ergo, this buyer had better deal with you, too. It's a point worth considering.

Going to the other extreme, a cheapie car is not so good either. To appear impoverished, unable to afford a decent car, can create the impression that you don't have much success in selling your watchamatronics, that people aren't buying them and that, ergo, there must be something undesirable about them .... Taking it by and large, as in so many other cases, the happy medium is the safest way to go.

18
THE LINE FOR THIS MONTH IS –

Getting the lead out

Everyone needs an occasional shot in the arm, a lift out of the humdrum, something to overcome the yawning, early morning blahs. There are those dog days when we drag our unwilling selves into our labors, prodding our flagging muscles, wishing something would occur to break up the everlasting monotony of work, work, work! Well – we can't do anything about eliminating the work other than by doing it. But –

There are such things as morning waker-uppers. Many nationally-known companies, recognizing the very human need for stimulation, resort, with surprising success, to some of the corniest of routines for getting the adrenalin moving in their employees. Like, they start the day out with group singing of old songs. They put on raffles. They create such things as circus atmosphere, with laugh-inducing, crazy costumes to be worn. And so on. It is hard to believe, but such presumably silly, childish rallies are tremendously effective in pepping people up for the day's work.

A rep firm is also made up of human beings, for whom generating enthusiasm, giving its members something "different" to go on, can prove even more rewarding. I'm not suggesting some kind of outlandish, jumping up and down performance. The *principle* of getting steamed up can be used – but in the form of a practical sales promotion. By combining that principle with a well-known, commercial practice, a program can be developed that will motivate and produce business. It's not nearly as complicated as it sounds:

We're all familiar with the widespread sales promotions

based on the customer subscribing to purchase a such-and-such on a monthly basis. This suggests an idea that can be applied to repping. Like so: for each month, select one line (or it could be a particular product) for *special* drive. Periodically, hold a morning sales meeting with your staff and announce, this is to be THE line for the month. Each member is to keep the chosen line uppermost in his thoughts, the first thing to talk about in making calls through the month to follow.

Go over the line's salient features. Have everyone concerned equipped with descriptive literature, samples and anything else you can think of pertaining to that line. Create the surging force of competition: offer a prize (preferably money!) to the man bringing in the most business on that line for the month, another for the man who has opened up new customers for it. The idea can be varied or enlarged upon to suit your own conditions; for example, you might want to put it on weekly instead of monthly.

Admittedly, there is nothing earthshaking about this procedure for getting all hands steamed up. (I'm told, some of the younger generation get the same results by using pep pills. About that, I wouldn't know!) Where you get the return is, first of all, such emphasis, such concentration, is bound to give the featured line real impetus. But aside from direct benefits, the special discussions and preparation entailed, the crossfire of ribbing and compliments as results are reported each morning, all makes for a change of pace. You're presenting something "different," a departure from the commonplace, a break in the ennui to which we are all, at one time or another, susceptible.

Give it a try – what can you lose?

19
THE THREE-CENT PENCIL

Last of the big spenders

Like so many businessmen who have had it, I long ago gave up giveaways. Customers become *so* blase about being handed those gadgets for their desks, pens, key containers, calendars and the like. You get a perfunctory, "Nice. Thank you" – and that's the end of it. What a waste of good money!

But I experienced one amusing and effective exception to my rule, however, which might hold some ideas for you. In order to get rid of a persistent solicitor in some good cause or other, I gave the fellow the order he wanted for a thousand pencils. They were only thirty dollars, imprinted with our company name, address and phone number – three cents per each.

When the pencils arrived, I tried to figure out what to do with them. To hand out such cheap things, I felt would be belittling and embarrassing. A silly thought occurred to me – at least, they might be good for a few laughs. I sharpened up a handful and stuck them in my lapel pocket.

On my first calls that day, I developed an act that later became regular routine. Each buyer got the same approach. Holding up one of the pencils, in a dramatic tone I would say, "Here is a very unusual, very special pencil. It is manufactured for only one particular purpose – that is, to write orders! Nothing else! It won't write anything else – just orders!" and I would hold it threateningly over his wastepaper basket or pretend to break it in two. "Well?"

Not only would I get the laugh worth the three cents but

frequently the guy would reach out and take it out of my hands, sometimes making some wisecrack of his own. It served as quite an ice-breaker with some of the withdrawn types who ordinarily presented a cold front, hard to penetrate. But, what became more significant – again and again, on subsequent calls, the buyer would grinningly produce my pencil, showing it *had* made enough of an impression to hang onto it. Sometimes he'd come up with a sally that he had evidently been preparing for me next time I showed, maybe about having saved it especially to write an order, slyly eyeing me to see the effect – which would draw from me a horrified, "Not for my competitors?" – and so on.

Just a little gimmick, at trivial cost, of the kind that produces one more bit of cement in the process of building friendly relationships, so invaluable to every rep. I have detailed it here only to prove that good will can be enhanced with simply slight departures from the usual, without necessarily laying out real money for costly, commonplace gadgets which the buyers don't appreciate.

20
ELEGY TO THE EXPEDITER

– a poem

Lives there a rep who has not said,
I wish to hell that guy was dead?

Aw, look, fellows – you've got to think of expediters like women. You can't get along with or without – etc. When that tough-talking guy calls to chew you out because he claims your delivery predictions make you a lousy prophet and rants on and on – console yourself. Keep your mind on the commission you're going to receive on the order he's spouting about and turn the valves down on your blood pressure.

Consider: you might be able to prove that (dirty word) is all wet by referring to your "order history record" (as previously described). *Could* be it will show the order is en route and about to be delivered any minute now. Maybe it's *already* delivered, as the invoice entry you have will show – thereby showing *him* up because his company's "receiving department" and "purchasing department" aren't on speaking terms. The information may be meandering through their in-house channels. He may not yet have the papers showing his precious order was received long ago. These things do happen!

But, so – maybe this time, he's right. The order is really overdue and what are you going to do about it, followed by unfeeling demands to spend your money on phone calls hurrying it up. But you could have forestalled his uproar. F'r instance: (hopefully) you were keeping that "Order History." Let's say you or one of your staff makes a habit of glancing over it each day, checking your order records for delivery schedules. If an order is going to be overdue, the fact will show up.

Whereupon, beat the expediter to the punch. Go after your factory immediately. *You* prod *them*. Get them off the dime or, at least, find out what's causing the delay, and for how much longer. And then – most beautiful gesture of all – *call your buyer* and tell him. (This is sometimes known as "service," the kind of for-real thoughtfulness that makes one rep stand out as a favorite to the buyers over another.)

Be prepared for the surprise of learning that, warmed by your solicitude, the tough guy turns out to be a nice fellow after all – just trying to make a living, like everybody else. He may be a bit grumpy at first, but he'll wind up taking your apologies and explanations graciously. He'll *thank* you for being thoughtful enough to forewarn him that his order is being delayed, so that he can plan accordingly. The *ill* wind is turned into a *good* will maker!

But, of course, that's a lot of trouble to go to. Maybe it's easier to work on finding new customers to supplant those lost because the customer is unhappy with the factory and, incidentally, with you because, you being the handiest, it's all your fault!

It's hard to accept the irritating fact that, having taken an order, you're only part way through. Instead of going on to more prospects, to use your energy for digging up more orders, you have to spend your time following up with the factory, keep checking on the order's progress, seeing to it that the order already taken is delivered. *You* have to become an expediter. How many jobs are you supposed to be doing? Does it make sense?

Yup! It do! You are not just a peddler, my friend. You are a manufacturers' *representative*! As such, you have to be a man of many parts, one of which is to be an arc in the circle that means completing the transaction you started.

21
YOUR IMAGE

Touching up the wrinkles

What forms that charisma which determines the desirability of one rep over another to the manufacturer? What, in the final analysis, determines a sales manager's choice when the process of elimination brings him down to two applicants for his line, both equally qualified?

Sometimes it's a very small, even trivial thing!

In considering the appointment of a new rep, sooner or later, the decision gets down to points so fine that sometimes they are overlooked by even some of our most experienced reps. One of these, functioning as a kind of frame for your image, is letterhead. Now, hold it! You, Mister Experienced Rep – just don't be too cocksure this is superfluous, too minor a matter, insofar as you are concerned. I've seen many old timers' rep letterheads whose shortcomings leave much to be desired – including some composed by professional industrial designers.

What kind of impression does your stationery make on the recipient? Let's say he's a sales manager. To him, you are a stranger, applying for his line. How you do business is only hearsay. He stares at your letter. Does it give him *all* the data which *should* appear on a piece of letterhead? For instance: it says in that broad, generic term, you are a "manufacturers' representative." But manufacturers of what? Plumbing supplies? Harness and saddles? What *do* you handle? Oh -- electronic products? Then why don't you say so?

Did you start your business yesterday? No – you're

established for many years? So why don't you incorporate that confidence-inspiring bit of data? Are you a member of some recognized trade or engineering association, a Chamber of Commerce? Those facts belong in there – exemplifying your firm as one of stability, of responsibility. How about the digits in your street address, phone number and so on? Are they pretty, very neat, in minimal type? Then, of course, you supply a magnifying glass with every letter you send out, so that the reader won't mistake a 3 for an 8 or a 9 for a 0 – don't you?

If you think these are silly questions, take a close look at *your* letterhead, Mister! Just spend a few minutes envisioning how much (or how little) it tells the sales manager who doesn't know you, but you wish he did! (I once represented a very experienced, long-time manufacturer who had to be awakened to the fact that his fancy, hand-lettered company name, and beautiful logo-decorated sheet of expensive letterhead failed to include his address! It's true, so help me! He had been using the stationery for two years – until the omission was pointed out to him!)

Now, about that special, hand-lettered logo: what's the difference between a drab, gray necktie and an attractive, colorfully designed tie? Do you want your company name unobtrusive, to be passed over casually, or is it more desirable that it hold the eye, at least long enough to make a good impression? Would you rather be a dull, retiring little businessman, or would you like to impress people with your personality, that you are a *somebody*?

Modern design, a thoughtfully laid out piece of letterhead, can tell much about you. I'll grant that symbols don't make a successful businessman but they sure as hell help convey the message. Making people *think* you're successful is in itself a good part of the battle.

A couple of words of warning about *who* does your letterhead. Your secretary? Does she know more about the business than you? How about leaving it up to the printer –

after all, that's his job, isn't it? Well, the run-of-the-mill "job shops" are seldom helpful when it comes to good design. In the main, their proficiency is limited to neat line-up of the copy you supply and making sure the ink is dry before they deliver the job.

There are, of course, large printing organizations who have excellent design departments. Even in that case, you'd better enter into what they're going to come up with and impose your judgment before it's too late. Nevertheless, unless you yourself are awfully good at this kind of thing (unusual among businessmen), these outfits are the best bet.

Finally, we have the so-called "industrial designer," the specialist. I've seen some beautiful examples of very intelligent work. But – I said, "some"! Watch out that you don't get tied in with one of these overly artistic types, who comes up with a "simply gorgeous" designed logo, with just bee-ootiful esthetic values – but what it stands for, only he knows! After all, portrayal of your image is intended for somebody's desk – not to be hung in a museum of modern art!

An even smaller thing – but only in physical size – is your calling card. While everything said heretofore about letterhead also applies to business cards, the latter is even more important because you hand them out to your customers – with the fervent hope that they'll keep 'em.

Get all the information on it that you can but *don't* list your lines on the back of the card. Show me a man who does that and I'll show you the world's champion optimist! Is there a rep who can truthfully say that, in any one year, he has not had a single change of lines? A deletion, an addition – probably more than one of each? Besides, this transparent economy has a cornball effect – it cheapens the looks of the card.

The doubled-over card is good. You've got more space to work with. It's protrusive; being thicker, it is more easily found in a file of cards. I often toyed with the idea of having a small version of my picture on the doubled calling card I used. I always passed up the idea – I'm still not sure why. It would be a distinctive addition to something which, obviously, is used for identification. There's nothing unusual about picturing oneself for commercial purposes. What's wrong with it? Does it appeal to you?

What I did do, however, was to employ a unique design for a doubled card that always drew unusual attention. On the upper portion there appeared only a facsimile of my signature; quite different from a simply printed name. It stood out. With plenty of white space available, I could pencil a little personal note like, "Hello – sorry you were out when I called today" – which made sure the receptionist would pass it on to my objective. It had other uses, such as jotting down an informal quotation or other notation before leaving the customer's desk, which would induce him to hold onto the card. Upon being bent open, the underneath section showed all the usual firm information, of course.

At any rate, the same thing holds true here as in the case of your letterhead – if the job is done cheaply, that's what it will look like. Cheap! Is that the kind of image you want?

Those triplicate speed forms – sure, fine! But – in their place! Like as inter-departmental communication between your office and the principal with whom you are firmly established. But for initial introduction, fine stationery is important. Actually, you will use very little of it – consequently, you can afford, and it should be only top class.

In addition to regular stationery, *all* printed matter you issue, whether form letters, lead cards, line rosters or what have you, should fix repeatedly on the same selected color, composition and type style, to establish identification at a glance even before being read. If you have done the piece with *class*, it will help convey the impressive status so important to the rep image.

22
SELF-CONSCIOUSNESS IS A CURSE

Dissolve it with five words

Self-consciousness is a miserable handicap to successful selling. Nothing so marks the novice – the hesitancy, the stammering, the shyness of approach, all add up to "amateur" and, in all probability, a nuisance. Noting the salesman's embarrassment, makes the prospect ill at ease. Trying to counteract and conscious of the poor impression he is creating, the salesman's voice may become harsh, forced, his manner aggressive to the point of belligerency.

Unfortunately, experience alone is not always enough to overcome the fault. Despite many years in the field, some men just don't achieve the poise, the state of equanimity, the correction of detracting personal characteristics that exemplify the *professional* salesman. Above all – but I can best illustrate what I am getting at by relating a couple of unique, personal anecdotes, a combination of traumatic experiences which resulted in a complete transformation in this writer's entire approach to the art of selling.

I was just leaving my teens, working for a small New York hardware manufacturer, whose main product was a "burglarproof" lock (and it was a good one). I served as a general office clerk, augmented by several weeks in the shop, making locks with my own hands. I knew that product!

How this manufacturer was to spread out from New York, to become nationally known, had become an uppermost subject for discussion by the management. The most logical territory for first expansion was nearby New England, where the lock was so far unknown. Various forms of advertising involved large expenditures for which the company was financially unprepared.

Someone suggested that *I* be sent up to the Boston area, there to do a missionary job, to familiarize the trade with at least the company's name and the product's features. After that, as finances permitted, a promotion campaign would be undertaken, to be followed up by some of their experienced salesman. The plan sounded good – while no one expected a kid like to me to take any actual orders, I could at least put in the initial background for the moves to follow.

At first, thoroughly alarmed, knowing my terrible shyness with strangers, I refused the assignment. They made it very plain. "You go – or else!" Jobs in those days were hard to come by. So, I went. I found myself a boarding house in Boston and dug in. Did I mention my youth – and the snide remarks, the insult to my vanity that I, though knowing the lock as I did, was not expected to actually sell any? Like hell, I vowed – I'll show 'em!

My bravado didn't last very long. Upon reaching the first dealer upon whom I was to call, I paced up and down the sidewalk outside of his store for over two hours! trying to summon up enough courage to enter! I thought of quitting – but I did need that job. When finally I managed to drag myself into the store, just as I expected, I stammered and blushed, trying to tell the dealer who I was and why I was taking up his valuable time.

Well, bless that man's soul, I guess he must have been young once himself because he listened tolerantly to my stumbling, introductory remarks. Encouraged by his forbearance, I dropped automatically into the virtues of the lock, on which I was myself so thoroughly sold. He began to show a little interest. Eventually, I all but ran out, clutching in my hot little hands a great big wonderful order for a quarter of a dozen locks! Wow! My first sale! Did I walk on air? I was flying way above Cloud 9! I thought of wiring my precious order in to the factory!

Now, highly elated, I decided to skip the small fry, to take on the biggest hardware dealer in the city. I girded up my loins. (I had them in those days.) I was ready to tackle lions. Unfortunately, it took about a half hour to get to my ambitious destination – long enough for my newly-found confidence to ooze away. When I arrived at the impressive establishment, I went through the same performance, pacing up and down outside, trying to get hold of myself, hoping against hope I wouldn't stammer this time when I talked with the big man. Finally, I dragged myself in and –

No dice! For the first couple of moments, the frowning buyer kept asking me to repeat, what was that I said my name was, what company did I represent? Finally, now completely tongue-tied, in diffident silence I handed him my calling card. His face lit up. "Hey!" he cried. "I know your company's lock – I've seen it in New York and it's a dandy. How come it's taken you people so long to get up here? Got a sample? How much? Tell me about them!"

Overwhelmed and delighted by this unexpected reaction, the pitch that followed became a torrent of words. (I told you I knew my subject, didn't I?) He slowed me down enough to write me an order for six dozen locks – a nice order even where we were known in New York. That one I did wire in to the factory, I was so excited.

But – the curse of self-consciousness stayed with me. Regardless, though I unbelievably sold locks to most of the territory on that trip, every call started the same way – and the curse continued to bug me, down through the years. Call it an inferiority complex or what have you – I only know that every initial meeting with a stranger started with my flushing, stammering introduction, dropping things, fumbling through the first introductory remarks. It continued through many varied business experiences. Once I got over the hump of preliminaries, I was all right – but oh, that beginning, that fear of confronting someone I had never met before.

I grew older. After some years in the automotive business, I was now a well-known radio parts distributor in Los Angeles. A trade association was putting on a prestigious affair, and I was invited to speak to the gathering, to comprise, as I learned later, something over five hundred men. When the proposal was first made to me, I could have swooned. Me? I? A guy who couldn't talk to even *one* stranger without making a fool of myself – to have to address a crowd like that? How preposterous can you get?

My friend, Norm N . . . . was the association's officer, delegated to handle the affair. Employing the selling tactics later to make him one of the country's most successful reps, Norm persuaded me, though however reluctantly, to give that talk. I wrote and practiced my speech for two weeks, until I could recite it forwards and backwards. Came the big night. As I drove toward the meeting auditorium with my wife, my courage melted away. If traffic had permitted, I would have turned back. But up ahead loomed the neon sign of a liquor store and I had an inspiration.

Though the era of prohibition had long ended, restrained by an old-fashioned bringing up somehow, up to this time, I had never got around to even tasting liquor. But, I had heard, whisky gives one courage. In desperation, I stopped and purchased a small bottle of bourbon. After turning the wheel over to my wife, I gulped down the entire contents. No use. The long ride, the cool, fresh air – I entered the hall and took my place with the other speakers, the blood in my veins like so much ice water.

Next to me sat Bill H. . . ., one of the well-known manufacturers' representatives of those days and a good friend of mine. Noting my pallor, Bill asked what was wrong. I admitted – I was scared to death of speaking to such a crowd. Bill was amused. Out of the depth of his experience, he scoffed at my fears. Then he made a curious comment.

"Frank," he said, "when I get up in front of a crowd like

this, I tell myself: the reason I was asked to talk to them is because I've got something to give them of value. When they are listening to me, *I'm* doing something for *them*. With that, I'm perfectly relaxed."

His words, seemingly so egotistical, made little impression on me. Things started. There were four speakers scheduled, to wind up with Dr. Lee DeForest, the distinguished guest of honor. The speeches were to be followed by a group of popular entertainers, their names and the famous inventor being the attraction that drew such a crowd. The orators droned on to wind up with the honored guest giving his talk about how he invented the audion. Norm, as the m.c., was about to bring on the eagerly-awaited professional performers. In that pregnant moment, he recalled that he had overlooked me!

With the audience audibly groaning in disappointment, I was introduced as the next speaker. It was ghastly – the temperature dropped to twenty below. I managed to make my way to the microphone, said "Ladies and gentlemen," and came to a dead stop. I had forgotten how my speech started!

For a long, very long eternity, the sullen crowd stared at me. Helplessly, I gazed at the ceiling. Finally, to bring the agony to a halt, I looked out at the audience and said,

"I had a fine speech prepared for tonight. Words that long," and my arms flung out, "interposed with bits of wisdom from the ages. I practiced it for two weeks, in my bathroom, in front of the mirror – with gestures, like this," and I sawed the air. "Folks, believe me when I tell you, it was a beautiful speech." I shook my head sheepishly and muttered into the mike, "Wish to hell I could remember how it started."

I heard a few snickers. Laughs sputtered from around the room; the audience broke out in a roar. First, I wanted to die, but, as I listened, I fell into laughing with them. "Oh well," I said, wiping my eyes, "like all speeches, mine had a joke in it. It's an old chestnut – guess that's why I remember it."

So, I told them my joke – which as it so happened was the second paragraph of the speech. The punch line got me my laugh and led me right along, smoothly, into what I had memorized. The audience now happily with me, I gained confidence, my voice lifted, the oratory resounded and I even wound up with an ad-libbed pun. In the uproar of applause, the great DeForest approached me with a sympathetic, "I know just how you felt. So often, I have been called upon to speak to an audience, not knowing what I was to say." Norm threw at me, "Liar! Thought you told me you never made a speech in your life!"

It was a moment of tremendous triumph, but – short-lived! With that, you'd think my self-consciousness would have become a thing of the past. Nope. No so. I continued to be the accursed, blushing violet, unable to overcome my initial shyness, my self-consciousness upon first meeting people. I was resigned to my doom, to living with the affliction for the rest of my life.

What creates that mental flash of lightning which we call inspiration? From whence does the power originate that motivates a brand-new thought? Is there anything more awe-inspiring than the processes of the human mind? Well, at any rate –

One evening, I was glancing through a book on business psychology. With increasing condescension, I read a paragraph devoted to the need for believing fully and conscientiously in the worth of one's product, of the self-confidence it would induce in demonstrating its virtues to a prospective buyer. A primer for school boys, I scoffed, as I tossed it aside. As though anyone calling himself a salesman doesn't know –

But it got me ruminating on the outstanding value of an exceptionally fine product which I was just then charged with introducing to a class of trade on whom I had never called before. My old bugaboo rose to worry me. I envisioned my problem in encroaching upon the busy, elusive buyers hiding behind their officious receptionists, the little pretties who consider it necessary to protect their bosses from those nuisance salesmen. I turned over in my mind the many advantageous features of this new product. Suddenly, I was beset by a new line of thought, and anger brought me sitting upright in my chair.

Why, I asked myself, must a reputable, knowledgeable salesman be diffident when faced with talking to a purchasing agent? Don't a seller's worthy product and a customer's usage of such products form the two sides of a coin? It came to me as a revelation, a ridiculously simple fact but, up to that moment, one that somehow had just never occurred to me: buyers *need* sellers.

With that, the entire philosophy of selling became sharply outlined in my mind. I saw that what I have in my brief case or behind my ears may be of incalculable value to a buyer's company. My brain raced. Bill H . . . .'s words came back to me. "Something of value to them . . . All they have to do is listen." For a few minutes of hearing me out, I might be saving that buyer's people large sums of money, or man-hours, perhaps supplying a device that would increase the efficiency of their operations. If he is a merchant, I bring products to him that could provide an opportunity for him to make money. Godamit, I swore out loud, why should I be so concerned about what the big man who allows me a few minutes of his time is doing for *me* when it is *I* who might very well be doing something important for *him*?

WHO'S DOING WHO THE FAVOR?

It was like an incantation. Those five words became engraved upon my mind, to forever put an end to the curse.

23
BUYING HOURS

Observing them leaves lots of time for golf

When I was repping, upon one occasion I had the opportunity of addressing a large group of industrial buyers. I vented my feelings about restricted buying hours by saying:

"We can't call on you on Monday because that's your day for getting the week organized. Friday is likewise out; you're too involved in wrapping up the week's work. That leaves us only three days of the week, during which we mustn't call on you before 9 a.m., when you are going through your mail. You're not available from 10 to 10:30; that's your coffee break. Between 12 and 2 p.m., you're away at lunch. After four o'clock, we don't dare call because you're too busy getting your paper work out and you're too damned tired for more salesmen anyway.

"That cuts the week to about 15 hours when we can see you – 10 of which we spend trying to find a place to park! Which reduces us to only five working hours a week to call on buyers – and that's why so many of you think a rep's life is a cinch!"

Well, they took my sarcasm good-humoredly because, despite the exaggeration, I wasn't too far away from the facts.

You're chomping at the bit, all enthused about hitting the ball, maybe ready to present a new line to the trade, just can't wait to tackle the buyers – and you're brought up short by the limitations of the customers' formal "buying hours." If you're a nice, polite boy, feeling you must defer to such mandates, and you conscientiously refrain from breaking the rules by confining your calls to the customers' eccentric variety of proscribed hours, you're going to have one helluva lot of unproductive time on your hands!

Of course, you're going to learn that some of these restricted "buying hours" are flexible – only guide lines, you might say, that can be disregarded with impunity. In-house friendships previously established, can help in overlooking the fact that you call at unauthorized hours. And there are such things as understanding, cooperative buyers, aware that the rep is important to their work, who don't mind your failing to see those forbodingly-worded "buying hours only" signs. Nevertheless, there are times when somebody is liable to ask you, "Can't you read?"

Circumventing these restrictions becomes part and parcel of every rep's life. Ingenuity may be required. Like diplomats, sometimes a rep has to follow a circuitous course to see his man. A certain rep of my acquaintance had a stock series of excuses for calling on a man at unorthodox times. It varied according to the circumstances and individual, but one of his most effective was receipt of a new catalog or a sample of a new product. He would deliberately refrain, say, from mailing the catalog at once but instead saved it – and especially if he had a new sample to show – for hand carrying to the buyer at odd hours, making the plausible-sounding explanation that such-and-such being so new, he just couldn't wait because he just *knew* the buyer would want to see it immediately – etc.

A drawing or a quotation for the buyer was made to order for him as a purpose for calling at unauthorized hours. Or he might offer as an apology for breaking in that he was going to be out of town for a prolonged period and he felt the buyer would want to give the subject matter early attention.

True, such practices lend themselves to abuse; transparent fabrications are liable to antagonize and may cause more ill will than good. You've got to know your man. In this writer's experience, the frank approach served best. I would phone the buyer, telling him how difficult it had been to get to him during his "regular" hours. Could he spare a few off-beat minutes? The response was very likely to be, "Sure, come on over" or perhaps he would name some mutually agreeable hour. I've never known a buyer who couldn't find time for exceptions to the company's buying rules if he is approached the right way. When you appeal to his good nature, you're playing on the fact that people like to appear helpful. And obviously, it makes a better call for you when you have the buyer's undivided attention, without him being conscious of the usual lineup in the reception office, waiting to get at him.

24
BY-PASS THE BUYER

It's a good trick if you can

As discussed in other chapters, there are basic differences between dealing with the "industrial" buyer and whoever does the buying for the "distributor." The rep calling on distributor trade rarely has the technology problems confronting the industrial rep. If the distributor doesn't act as his own purchasing agent, he will have delegated this function to someone experienced in merchandising, the finer technical points of the goods he stocks being of lesser concern.

It's not like that for the industrial rep.

How curious is the kind of economy which makes industrial "buyers" of men who cannot possibly have accumulated *both* the product knowledge and the wisdom required to intelligently handle hundreds of thousands, even millions of their companies' money. It is trite to say not all buyers are the same. However, there are all too many who, though personable, often college graduates and mentally bright enough, simply have not had enough time on earth to accumulate the experience they should have. They are supposed to properly evaluate the often highly technical, widely varied products with which they are confronted all day long. In addition, at the same time, they are assumed to be sufficiently versed in the laws of economics to expend vast sums of money wisely. That's asking a lot of a man. Yet, that's the way it is. I dunno. It seems to work. Anyway, regardless, the rep has to contend with anything from "pencil pushers" on out through the debatable degrees of intelligence exhibited in purchasing departments.

Whatever may be the extent of the buyer's competency,

the industrial rep should use every means, every dodge, all his wits to circumvent the buyer, to deal initially with the engineers. Once the buyer has a requisition on his desk, the deal is way downstream. He will buy what the originator of that requisition calls for. Hence, it is up to you to see that *your* products are named therein accordingly.

Sometimes this order of things is easy. It depends on company policy and the individual buyer. One, aware of his limitations, will wave you on freely with a "Go see our engineers – they tell me what to buy." Great! Go, and pitch!

Another buyer, protecting his job, jealous of his prerogatives, will bristle at the suggestion of talking with the engineers. With this guy you're in trouble. You'll just have to do the best you can.

Sometimes short-sighted, even stupid, policy on the company's part makes it a rule that reps must call only on the buyer. "That's what we pay buyers for," management storms. "Leave our engineers alone." Just how such companies expect their engineers to keep up with the latest, applicable products, enabling them to utilize some newly developed component particularly effective for their purposes, is a moot question.

Of course, despite working closely with the engineers, you don't neglect the buyer – heaven forbid! After all, he might be and probably would be the last word. Let him know who you are with everything you've got. Even the buyer who so obligingly refers you to his engineers, must not be neglected. If you submit quotations to the engineers, be *sure* the buyer receives duplicate copies, and cater to him – don't ever let *him* get the feeling that you are bypassing him. Even though he is good-naturedly acquiescent, make a point of asking his permission before seeing the engineers. You've just got to keep him happy – because that's what your competitor is doing!

I can't leave this subject without speaking of one notable exception to customary buying methods, a major instrument manufacturer whose reputation is world famous, who became cognizant of the foregoing problem several years ago and decided to do something about it. They inaugurated a unique purchasing system which, though highly successful, oddly enough has not spread to other manufacturers.

Basically, it began with the startling ruling that reps were henceforth forbidden to call on their buyers. Not that the buyers were abolished; instead, the company set up senior engineers, each one heading up a group in his particular product category. The routine became simple: when a rep had a new product to offer, he was instructed to call this group leader on the phone, give a brief explanation of the product and request an interview. Unless it was one which could not possibly be of interest, a definite appointment would be made and they would get together.

Then, upon carefully reviewing what the rep had to offer, the senior might say, "This is a good item but it has no application in our work," and that would be the end of it. On the other hand, if he thought the product had even slight possibilities, he would tell the rep, "I'll take it up with my engineers." And he *would* do exactly that. If one or more of his group evinced interest, the rep would soon receive a phone call, telling him *which engineer* to see and when.

This done, literature, samples and quotes left, an order could follow, made out and signed by a buyer whom the rep had never seen, whose name he might not even recognize!

It was a system made successful because the *right* people become cognizant of a new item, without wasting time of others in a huge organization who might otherwise pass the item up because it was of no particular interest to them. From the rep's standpoint, the situation was good because, for the same time-saving reason, it led him directly to the individual who understood his product and was capable of determining its usage for his company. Obviously, this system made of the senior engineer a high-priced buyer but, again, gives graphic evidence that you get what you pay for.

25
ON PLAYING SANTA CLAUS

Must you advertise your competitor?

Every rep has his own preferred way of making a presentation when calling on a prospect who is considering a device entirely new to his operation. However, there is one selling fault to which even the most experienced salesman is susceptible because it is so insidiously subtle. I think it might be worth a bit of discussion.

To say a salesman should know everything possible about his competition is to simply repeat one of the ABC's of selling. But unfortunately, the ambivalent state of being so all-fired knowledgeable about the competition, can create the possibility of selling a competitor's product at one's own expense. It is a paradoxical situation that may occur because, when the competition weighs heavily on your mind, it can readily slip down to the tip of your tongue.

What can then ensue is that, in extolling the virtues of your product to the prospective buyer, you compare it to the other fellow's, believing you are making points for your offering as against his. But it is entirely possible that the prospect knows little or nothing about your competiton. Why awaken him to a source of supply other than yourself?

Or, suppose he has heard about your competitor's device. The very fact that it is being used by *you* as a standard for comparison, piques his interest. You've enhanced its importance just by bringing it up. The inference is conveyed that you, presumably an expert on such things, have a lot of respect for the other fellow's product since you seem to find it necessary to make comparisons. Which gets the prospect thinking: maybe he'd better look closely into this other deal – and he stalls you off accordingly.

Know what points you should stress in order to offset the competitor's product but *don't name it*! Don't mention it if you can possibly help it. If the prospect brings it up, just shrug it off with a brief generalization about competition and go back to what *you* want to talk about. Leave it to the other fellow to promote his own interests. Don't do it for him! So far as you know, there is only one product in the whole great big wide world and that is the one *you* are selling.

26
STORY OF A TOOTHACHE

A fulfilling experience

Many a salesman has run across some effective wrinkle, some unusual twist or other that worked for him in nailing down an order. But what can an old-time, lifelong salesman learn about *goodwillship*, if you will – a method by which a one-time customer can be made into a *repeat* customer? Can you teach an old dog new tricks? Thereby hangs a unique, recent incident. I wish it had happened when I was repping. I'd have put it to good use.

In my part of the country (and yours, too, I'll bet) dentists seem to be the busiest men around. Barring emergencies, and sometimes not even then, you've got to make appointments weeks, and sometimes months in advance, to get their services. Right?

For a number of years, my wife and I had been going to a certain dentist, one whose personality was not exactly fetching. He had an abrasive, autocratic way of running his patients in and out of his chair, without much regard for social amenities. Charges for his service steadily escalated. Well, I would sigh, what can you do – good dentists are hard to find and I guess they all charge the same these days, they're in such demand.

A nagging, intermittent ache had developed in one side of my jaw. This dentist located a tooth he decided needed filling. Upon finishing the job, he said I might have some discomfort for a week or so but that the pain would gradually subside. And, he sent me the usual big bill. But months passed, and the aching condition continued. I went back. He scraped, poked around, said he could find nothing wrong, to "try it a little longer." For that, he billed me ten bucks.

Well, that did it! Come hell or high water, I vowed, I'm finding me a new dentist. It took time, but finally I located a well-recommended man. He X-rayed, explored and prodded. "Got it," he announced. "It's a bit of decay back of that crown there." He cleaned it out and filled it.

Upon leaving his office, for the first time in many months, I was free from toothache – but *that's* not the point of the story. About nine o'clock that very same evening, my new dentist phoned me at home. "How are you feeling?" he asked. "Any bleeding? Any swelling? No? Well, I just wanted to make sure. Don't hesitate to let me know if you have any discomfort between now and your next appointment. Good night."

Need I say, I was flabbergasted? Long after I received his very reasonable bill, to everyone who would listen, I waxed eloquent about this uncalled-for, astonishing, extra-curricular example of concern about me and my welfare.

As a rep, you and your customer have sweated your way through a deal. It may or may not have entailed considerable time and attention from both of you but it was an important project to your customer. Eventually, the order came through. It was shipped, billed, paid for, the transaction duly completed.

Then, suppose – just *suppose* you gave your customer a ring and asked him, was the factory's service okay, the goods as represented? Everything work out to his satisfaction? Good Lord – wouldn't that man be surprised, knowing you were through with the deal, your commission collected? Wouldn't he be delighted to learn that you were *still* concerned, that *you* wanted to make *sure* you had done right by him? Can you imagine how that guy would be singing your praises, just as I have with my dentist? And above all, think of the welcome you would receive the *next* time you called to solicit his business!

Think about it!

27
SECRETARIES

Enter sexcess; exit success!

Despite the hoary, ubiquitous jokes and wifely suspicions, I don't think the level-headed businessman of today needs to be admonished about the hazards of employing the predominantly sexy gal as a secretary. If he has reached any degree of maturity at all, he knows that sexcess can defeat success, that if normal relations with his secretary extend into the extra-curricular, his wife won't like it and, besides, the business ownership can change hands – instead of the gal working for him, it could wind up with him working for her! To say nothing of how the protrusive, aesthetic values of an attractive girl can arouse the artistic appreciation of other (male) employees, to distract them from the mundane duties of their jobs.

Nor have I any intention of holding forth about sex, per se. One reaches that plateau in life when a good looking gal just goes in one eye and out the other, when such subject matter consists pretty much of fading pictures hanging in the more musty museum section of one's memory. Well, let's see – sorry – my mind got to wandering. Let's get back to business.

The younger girls working in an office have their points (or curves, if you prefer, and they are old enough). They're apt to be alert, easily trained, tractable and modest in their salary demands. But propelled by inevitable time, they tend to be transient. The young woman changes jobs for what will strike you as capricious reasons. Over the phone, her neophyte uncertainty or, even worse, youthful flippancy and couldn't-care-less attitude, can drive customers away. The urgencies of your business needs are secondary to dates in her mind. Sooner or later, you'll lose her via the marriage route. If she continues working after marriage, the likelihood of pregnancy speeds her departure.

As a secretary, you will be wise to try for the mature, experienced, responsibility-assuming woman. The older one is likely, in most cases, to be thoughtful, have better poise and be more zealous in her work than the youngster. When talking with customers on the phone, instead of those exasperating, impersonal rejoinders, she will know how to convey cordiality and concern. Her self-assuredness, stemming from years of familiarity with the businessman's thinking, helps inspire confidence in the firm.

She will be cognizant of the necessity for keeping the phone *alive*. When she tells the caller for you that you'll soon be on the phone, she doesn't leave him hanging there in long, deadly silence because you don't answer promptly. Haven't *you* had that experience when *you* are the caller? You wait for your man – and you wait and wait. *Is* the gal ringing him? Has she forgotten you? Are you still connected? What the hell goes on there, anyway? No, a good secretary will keep coming back at short intervals to keep the impatient caller placated until you answer.

Needless to say, phone personality is a prime requisite in a good secretary. (I am reminded of a rep who chuckled in relating how often, when he happened to answer the phone himself, the customer would kid him, saying, "I don't want to talk with you – lemme speak with Mamie – *she* knows what she is talking about!" How blessed is the rep with a secretary capable of creating this kind of reputation with his trade.)

You've probably watched that long-standing TV program "What's My Line?" At some point, the blindfolded panel must guess the identity of some famous personality. Though usually a professional actor, no matter how effectively the guest attempts to disguise his voice, in short time the panel knows who he is. Something of a revelatory characteristic, no matter how small, gives him away.

It shows how sharply attuned the ear is to the human voice. It behooves you, too, to pitch your voice at warmly receptive frequencies instead of giving the caller the feeling that he is intruding upon your state of tranquility. If you insist, and rightfully so, that your secretary answer the phone in a pleasant, welcoming manner, should you be different?

And another thing about phonecons – such a small but thoughtlessly common irritation: your girl has asked the caller's name; he perhaps has had to spell it out for her. She calls you to the phone, *telling* you in advance what the man's name is. You come on with a mere "Hello" – and he has to go through the process of confirming that you are you, and identifying himself all over again. Why can't you respond with whom you are and address the caller by his name, to get the conversation promptly on its way?

If you are not aware of your own telephone shortcomings (like maybe you don't talk into the transmitter is another irritating possibility), ask some friend who has occasion to call you at your office once in a while, to give you a frank criticism of your phone personality. You might be surprised.

An inept secretary is going to waste much of your time and cause you plenty of trouble. Ergo, it pays to take *lots* of time *before* you hire the gal. Go beyond simply a perfunctory interview and typing test. Enquire *thoroughly* into her past experience. Don't take an employment agency's word for it – they're trying to sell her. Have *her* type up a resume *in your office*, with periods of previous employment clearly set out (in itself a good typing test). Watch for the breaks in job periods – how often does she change employers? Be sure and call former employers for reference purposes; it is surprising how many reps neglect to obtain this potentially revealing information.

Being feminine, of course the applicant will be neatly dressed. No spots will appear on her clothing because that would be a sure revelation of careless habits. Study her *finger nails*; are they clean, giving evidence of care? If a woman doesn't give reasonable attention to her own person, what can you expect in the way of attention to the details of *your* work?

When dictating a letter to test her typing, don't make it too complex. Allow for the applicant's nervousness. Many applicants stress their typing speed but it's *accuracy* that's much more important in the rep business. Introduce some common words, of a kind frequently misspelled, like "amateur," "professional," "mathematics," "bookkeeping," "embarrassment" and such. (Leave a dictionary handy; if she resorts to it, that can be a sign of her desire to be accurate in what she does.)

Don't tell her where to paragraph – let her figure it out for herself. (Such spacing can indicate the ability to understand the subject when you speak to her as well as how to nicely arrange a letter's appearance.) Try giving her the essential facts and let her compose a letter herself. (Some girls can turn out a better letter than the boss.)

If you are impressed with the desirability of an applicant, don't haggle with her over the amount of remuneration. You may have to pay an exceptional gal more than you think you can afford but the difference between an efficient secretary and the run-of-the-mill office girl just can't be measured in dollars. If she's good, she'll bring back the money she costs many fold.

The man who claims he can't afford a capable secretary might program this into his abacus: how much time does he spend in the office, doing work which a good girl can do? Say the going rate in his area for such a gal is four bucks or so an hour. Can an experienced sales engineer afford to sell his services for that kind of money? Because, isn't that what he's doing when he keeps struggling along without a good secretary?

If you're lucky enough to have a girl whose services are worthy of appreciation, let her know it. It's her nature to feel needed. Compliments are more important to the feminine mystique than to a man. And don't wait for her to ask for a raise. Sooner or later, the subject is bound to come up. Beat her to it – the impact will be greater than if she had to ask for it. And small raises at frequent intervals are more effective in keeping a girl happy on her job than making her wait a long time for a major raise.

Having wound up with the women in your business life, I am reminded of a personal incident: a friend visiting us at home, commented on the incongruity of the reading matter he saw lying on my easy chair. "Well," I explained, "the Wall Street Journal is for considering the future. The copy of Playboy is for thinking about the past. But you see that heating pad? That's for the present!"

Next chapter, please!

28
PENNY PINCHERS

A hundred pennies still equal a dollar

Busy men have a way of turning over the purchasing of office supplies to their secretaries. The amounts involved are small. It is commonly believed that a woman is a sharper buyer than a man. Mebbe so. It often depends on whose money she's spending. Now, you take those nickel-and-dime office supplies:

Large stationery houses employ outside salesmen. They're apt to be the kind who "have a way with women." They also have innumerable new items from time to time, outside of the usual staples, of a special nature (usually with better than standard mark-up!). It is their salesmen's jobs to cajole, to use every blandishment by way of persuading the girl buyer to order these things. Sometimes the thingamajig is an excellent adjunct to her work. More often, it is used once or twice, eventually to join a similar conglomeration of junk in one of her desk drawers.

What about your printed matter? That's a crazy business. I've never known two printers to quote the same on a given job – they seem to vary all over the lot. You'll do well to shop around. BUT – what's the point of dwelling on such minor matters? Well, for one thing, the reasoning applies to every office expenditure. And that brings up a question:

Suppose, by sharp buying, you can save a couple hundred bucks a year on overhead? How much sweat and toil do you have to expend before you make a *commission* of two hundred dollars?

Set up a formula. Then, translate the amount of each expenditure as it comes up in terms of how much business you have to do to offset it. You won't necessarily be negative but you will find yourself closely questioning the purpose and presumed benefits of every dollar your office spends – and that's good business!

29
CALLS WITH YOUR SALESMAN

Surprise, surprise!

Once, a long time ago, when I was rather young to be a distributor, I received a piece of invaluable advice from a wise old head, which, much to my later regret, I didn't take. I pass it on to you here, in the hope that if you employ salesmen, you will make a better use of it than I, who had to learn the hard way:

This man, one of the country's best known manufacturers, was seated at my desk, gazing quizzically at the piles of papers scattered about. We had been speaking of the differences in results between outside salesmen. "How often do you get out in the field with your men?" he asked.

"Me?" I looked at him in disgust, pointing to the work piles. "Who's got time?" I snorted. "Anyway – what do you think I'm paying those guys for?"

"That's a mistake," he replied earnestly. "It's not that you should accompany the man to do the selling for him. But you'd be surprised at what you will learn, just tagging along once in a while."

"So?"

"A salesman reporting always glosses over his own shortcomings. He'll present excuses for losing the order which still shows *him* in a favorable light, whereas the customer might give *you* an entirely different explanation, proving that in some way or other, something your man does or doesn't do, costs you the business.

"You'll detect mannerisms in your man's approach to the customer which could be detrimental. You may find the buyer with whom the salesman claims to be buddy-buddy, scarcely knows your guy exists. The customer, in recognition of your superior position, may come out with information which he doesn't bother to give to a "hired hand."

"You'll pick up details at first hand, when you yourself are present at an interview with a prospect, which you probably wouldn't learn otherwise. Not the least benefit is that some buyers are flattered to be considered important enough for the boss to be calling on them in person. And on the other hand, if your man is doing a good job, you'll become aware of just why, maybe to help you pass his methods along to others of your staff."

I shrugged. Only later, after many unhappy circumstances, did I wish I had started to follow his advice immediately. Like one day, I had a call from a customer, complaining about an error on one of his orders. Trying to understand the details, I asked what he had specified to Tom So-and-so, the salesman, when the order was taken.

"Tom?" exclaimed the customer. "I haven't seen him around here in months! I phoned that order in."

After hanging up, I checked over Tom's call reports. They indicated he had called regularly on this account every week, over the past several months. When I finally got to the bottom of the situation, I learned this guy habitually sat himself down at his home phone every morning, called the customers on the phone and wrote up his reports and occasional orders as though he had actually been there! Within an hour or so, he had done his job and would have the rest of the day for his favorite pastime, which was chasing women.

On another occasion, I received a call from a competitor. He was in a howling rage, roaring out that one of my salesmen had been spreading a story among customers all over the territory to the effect that this competitor was headed for bankruptcy. By way of witness, one of his own salesmen had stood in the background, listening to my idiot popping off to the customer.

When I put the stupe on the carpet for his big mouth, he looked at me in surprise. "Why," he said, "I thought everybody knew that. I heard he was going through an IRS audit, that he was going to be hit with a penalty that was going to break him. I forget who told me but everybody knows about it" – etc., etc. Only the fact that this competitor and I happened to be personal friends, enabled me to stop a libel suit.

Then there was the salesman who was quoting from a list of prices on one of our best moving lines, somehow unaware of the quantity discount schedule applicable, and wondering why he wasn't getting the sizable orders on it that the other men were bringing in. Since he had been doing well enough over all on the other lines, it was a long time before I caught up with that situation.

Yes, those were my salad days – one lives and learns. But don't think such things happen only to a naive young businessman. Just very recently, I learned of an incident wherein a very experienced rep took over the accounts of one of his salesmen who had quit the job. Talking with a buyer who had been buying one of their lines in large quantities, this rep mentioned another very important line and asked why the buyer had never shown interest in it. His jaw dropped when the buyer replied, this was the first time he knew the rep had the referenced line! The salesman, presumably content with the nice business he was already getting, had never brought up the subject of the other line with the account! The rep walked out with an order right on the spot.

Yup, I could give you many more examples of why I learned how important it is for "the boss" to show himself at the customer's place once in a while. Of course, you don't make the call *without* your salesman. Obviously, he would become very unhappy at what would look like a sneaky way of checking up on him. But I do say, get out on calls with him occasionally. And just invite yourself along on spur-of-the-moment days, without allowing any special preparation – and see what happens. Mister, you'll learn things that will surprise you, I guarantee! Yup – you'll learn.

30
LETTERS TO PRINCIPALS

The long and short of it

Some sales managers demand all but daily letters from their reps, far beyond reasonable reports on "what cooks." They want to know you're working! Others don't want to be bothered with anything except orders. What's the happy medium? How much time can you – *should* you – expend on letter writing?

We can assume that urgent matters are attended to by phone or wire. But some situations require more detailed discussions, best handled by mail. As a common example: you're on an important deal, with several individuals and a variety of influential factors involved. Need for the factory's help comes up.

Under those conditions, some reps write lengthy, fully detailed letters about it to the factory. They conscientiously spell out the names of all the buyers and engineers concerned along with their respective departments, and describe the conversations with the customers' management about the deal. They fill in with deep background, going on and on, bringing out every facet of the subject.

To what purpose? Why obscure the essential facts in a wearying mass of superfluity? Why take the time? What is accomplished?

As the girdle put it, there should be a limit to everything.

There is another aspect to writing highly detailed, though not necessarily boring letters, but self-defeating. Once, in the days before I learned better, I received an effusive, most complimentary letter from one of my sales managers, telling me my thoroughly informative letters made him feel as though he were right on the customers' front doorsteps. Later, when I no longer had the line, *I* stood on the doorsteps, mournfully watching another rep march right in, fully armed with specific information from the factory, to pick up the deals for which I had so nobly prepared the way.

Some reps believe they are being impressive, that they are doing a good job for the principal in writing him all such details about customer situations. So? How wise is it for a rep to establish a beautiful file on the trade back at the factory – so very convenient and helpful for the next rep who takes the line over, to pick up the marbles if, as and when the aforesaid rep is terminated?

Sure, it cuts both ways. You do need help from the factory – technical information, delivery availability, pricing to meet competition. Obviously, the factory needs the applicable data. All right – but confine your letter to just producing enough answers for *you* to pass on to the customer. Don't make the mistake of thinking you're saving time and energy by placing the factory in direct contact with the customer because it can lead to the question, what do they need *you* for? Besides, information can pass between the buyer and the factory of which you may not be made aware at the time – later, in your ignorance, making you look stupid.

In other words, my friend, service is one thing – but there is a point of no return. To be a hero, to give for free of your time, your know-how, your competence – well, the Peace Corps is a wonderful, worthy cause.

On the other hand, you have the man who writes letters as though they cost like telegrams – frustrating, incomprehensible notes, leaving the recipient at a loss to properly understand the subject matter. The business world's pendulum has swung away from rhetoric, from polite and verbose mannerisms, from such redundant phraseology as, "Yours of the 29th instance was received today wherein you state that" – and, "in response I hasten to respond by –" and so on. But in its place, brevity has become a fetish. What price economy of language if a misunderstanding is created by lack of clarity due to insufficient words, and if you have to write a second letter by way of explaining what you should have said in the first place?

It is a deplorable fact that many men who, admittedly, studied *literature*, in college, somehow missed learning usage of *English* in a way that would enable them to communicate intelligibly with their fellow men. We have at our disposal the world's richest language. Even scholars can do no more than guess at its extent, estimates varying from something like a half million to several million words, with no two declared to have precisely the same meaning. Yet, so many of us employ a vocabulary of no more than a few thousand words.

How much better we might get along with our fellow creatures if we were able to express exactly what we want to say and if, in turn, our listeners understood our words' complete meaning. But, the realities of daily existence make it necessary, as always, to compromise, to adapt ourselves to the conditions that pertain. For the harried, time-short businessman, clarity in the fewest possible words must be his aim. Literate usage of language is to be desired, of course, but what he *means* is the crux of his letter writing – not necessarily *how* he says it.

It is a matter of choice but, in this writer's opinion, an effective letter strikes a note between so-called formal business English and social correspondence. In other words, as I see it, you "take it easy." You don't strain for words you wouldn't use face-to-face. You avoid stiff, formal language because stilted phraseology makes one sound cold, distant. You let your personality come through. There can be times when a pungent bit of slang or a colloquialism here or there can make the subject matter more meaningful than if you were to confine yourself to pedantic English. In short: you write the way you talk, so long as you stay reasonably concise.

No need to go into the costs of writing a business letter. We all know figures on this chore can run up to three dollars a letter because many factors enter into such writing beyond the cost of stationery and a stamp. Yet, letters must be written. For some men, it would take a course in English to learn how to write a succinct and yet comprehensive letter. For any interested in pursuing this point further, of the innumerable books available on the subject, "The Art of Readable Writing" by Rudolph Flesch is one of the best.

31
SALES MANAGERS

It takes all kinds

It is within the sales manager's powers to make the rep's life a bed of roses or delegate him to sleeping on the floor. Since it becomes necessary to acknowledge the sales manager is human (although even that distinction sometimes becomes a bit blurred), we must perforce accept his frailties along with his contributions to our well being. He may introduce distortions in the image of being your own boss but, like the man who chooses the right parents, fortunate indeed is the rep who has the guiding influence of good sales managers.

So what makes a "good" sales manager? Is he the one who leaves you strictly alone, to do your thing as you see fit – just send him orders? Not the character who is always on your back, demanding bigger and better business? Well, sales managers have their quirks and idiosyncracies. They come in all varieties of the Homo Sapiens. Some are weaklings, others fire-eaters. What rep doesn't have stories of the stupidly destructive one or the intelligently helpful sales manager? To enter into the degrees of competency among these men, would entail a study of the human race. All we can do is highlight here and there, the effect of the individual sales manager upon the rep, recognizing that while the sales manager is in the driver's seat, it is the rep who supplies the power that makes the car go.

In making our judgments, we must allow that there are really no defined, well precedented courses for the sales manager to follow. In one sense, he may be looked upon as a glorified version of the rep. He establishes his own pattern for doing his job. As the rep operates between customers and principals so, too, is the sales manager a man in the middle – teetering between his own superiors who expect profitable results and, on the other hand, working with his reps, a bunch of highly individualistic characters, widely varying in experience, competence, personality. Among the qualifications which denote a "good" sales manager, unquestionably foremost is the need for a profound understanding of human nature. But in innumerable other ways, the requirements for successful sales managership are rigorous, indeed.

It has become a cliche to describe a "good" sales manager as one who has been himself a rep. Presumably, such a man understands the rep's problems. But it doesn't *necessarily* follow that a man is skilled in managing others simply because he was once a salesman himself. To be an able sales promoter from a commanding position, calls for more than just firing line experience – much more. There are many soldiers but few are qualified to become generals.

You'll forgive me if force of habit has me using the term "sales" manager – by which, of course, I am broadly covering the "marketing" manager. That brings to mind the noticeable increase in the number of young men, college educated in marketing management. So far, however, most of the managers seem to be drawn, in one way or another, from the ranks of business experienced men. Among these are manufacturers who, in the course of building their enterprises, function as their own sales managers. And some of the last named do all right, too.

Story of a master brain-picker

Like my contemporaries, I have at various times represented some of industry's nationally famous, multi-million-dollar companies, operated by highly organized, presumably top-flight management. Ergo, it may seem curious that I would select as the most *effective* sales manager I ever knew one who headed up a comparatively small factory, having no background of real selling experience himself, who functioned as his own sales manager, knowing nothing more about the business when he started than how to make his quite prosaic products.

This man's initial qualifications appeared to be few. His past held no more than a typical kid's selling jobs. He had only a high school education. He had no particular personality charms. Nevertheless, that man, in the course of the years, built up a solid business, with a national sales organization that included a number of the country's best known reps. They made money on his line and he, himself, became successful enough to retire before what most would consider middle age. Luck? Miracles? An outstanding proprietary product that everybody just had to buy?

Nope. None of those things. It began when he was knocking out a living, operating a small machine shop. He happened to pick up a job lot of supposedly junk dies. Upon sorting them out, some proved to be intended for making certain simple electronic components. He made a few inquiries, learned the function of these devices and that they were in widespread use. He studied the brands currently sold. His shop developed a slightly improved version of these devices. Because of the somewhat better design, orders came easily.

He expanded, building up a line with other compatible items. But prompted by the example of his first products, he operated on a restricting principle to which he doggedly adhered from the very beginning, namely, to feature quality rather than price. He tried to do his own selling. He was without sales promotion experience, and was singularly lacking in the polish, the ebullient personality ordinarily associated with the salesman. Progress was slow.

The break came when he learned a system of professional salesmen existed, men available to help market his products, whom he did not have to add to his payroll – i.e., the rep! Not only that, but he found the know-how of these independent manufacturers' representatives could be utilized for the instruction, the consultation he so desperately needed. In time, he acquired a roster of reps across the country and that is where his genius (if such is what you want to call it) became manifest.

That man was the greatest brain picker I ever met! Even in later, prosperous years, he never ceased asking questions. Always uppermost was his desire, his anxiety to learn. He sought out the pros, the knowledgeable men in the trade, and he applied what he learned from them. He knew that people are flattered when you bow to their experience and ask their advice – you'll always get it.

Let me cite just one example of his understanding of human nature and why, down through the years, he developed such outstanding rapport with his reps, to the benefit of all concerned. On one of his frequent field trips, I was showing him a looseleaf binder compilation devoted entirely to his now widely known, greatly expanded line. It was organized in sections arranged and tabbed to separate catalogs, drawings, advertising reproductions, competitors' literature, price sheets and so on. It was a very complete presentation and he was extremely complimentary about it.

"You can take this along as a model for your reps, if you wish," I offered magnanimously. "I can make up another one."

"No!" he shot back decisively.

My vanity considerably deflated by his abrupt refusal, I asked, "Why?"

"I give you guys salable products. My prices are competitive. Deliveries are reasonable. I provide all the literature you ask for. I back you up with a good advertising program. I exhibit at all the major shows. Correspondence is answered promptly. My commission rate is good. In short – my reps have a good line to work – right?"

I agreed. "But," I argued, "this binder compilation is of outstanding usefulness for a rep – you just said that yourself. Why not see that they make up such a tool?"

"Because you characters are individualists – that's why you're reps. You all have your own ways of selling and you're the pros – I don't know how and I don't try to tell you how to sell."

"But suppose – "

He continued, "If a rep gets me results, I leave him alone."

"And if not?"

"I fire him and get myself another rep!"

To me, that experience has always been a wonderful example of a manufacturer who not only had the acumen to understand reps, but took full advantage of all the independent manufacturers' representative system offers. As a result, everybody came out ahead.

A big-hearted principal

This is just an unimportant but little human interest anecdote whose outcome illustrates a sad situation sometimes confronting the rep. One of the oddest sales managers I ever knew was, also, the manufacturer himself. He must have been the world's busiest, hardest-working man. All I had to do was to mention the name of a new prospect on whom I had made my first call, and Mr. M. would take over. The day he heard about a prospect from me, a voluminous letter would go out to the lead, extolling the virtues of the factory's products. In short order, the prospect would get a phone call from him, soon followed by another, with more letter follow-ups. Sometimes he even got the order direct.

This happened again and again. It bothered me. One day,

in the course of a phonecon with Mr. M. I said, "I don't mind your doing my work for me, so long as you keep sending those nice, fat commission checks. Trouble is – this is too good to last."

"You don't want me to contact the customer?"

"Only through me," I replied firmly. "Let me do it. I know these people better than you – "

I could almost see him beam. "It's quite refreshing," he said, "to have a rep who wants to earn his commission."

"If he doesn't," I said self-righteously, "I know damn well the commissions will soon dwindle or stop."

We got along first rate after that – for a while. Since this is a true story, I must tell you the end. Quite unexpectedly, he put on a sales manager – who, it just so happened, was a relative of his.

Need I tell you the rest? Long after I had to resign the line, I used to think of Mr. M, wondering why such a nice, well-meaning guy, had to take on the support of his relatives, as well as doing his reps' work.

The young marketing manager

Given the gigantic, multi-billion dollar industries of today, one now rarely hears the once ubiquitous cliche, "Such-and-such a business is still in its infancy". From the horse-and-buggy age, not altogether forgotten, modern industry's phenomenally swift growth still includes a dwindling though vigorous number of pioneers, fully active in its progress. But, of necessity, its corresponding multiplication of personnel has drawn to it a vastly diversified mixture of individuals, with varied and sometimes debatable talents.

The highly publicized, graphic attempts of youth to change long-standing social structures has taken older generations aback, though many elders secretly or openly hope the kids' efforts will, indeed, make of this a better world. Whether one approves or not, we have with us the cult of youth –

which, however, didn't start yesterday. For many years now, the business portion of the world has been placing young people in the higher positions once reserved for the middle-aged and elderly. The dilemma of trying to achieve the benefits of youth despite the exacting need for experience, has resulted in some curious instances of long practiced businessmen having to deal with equals or superiors young enough to be their sons.

The enthusiasm, the fresh mentality, the springy muscle of youth, are advantages particularly appropriate for this continually expanding, fast-moving technology of today. Coupled with college education in marketing procedures, it is not hard to see why a manufacturers' ownership may be carried away, to select a young man for a position of authority over hard-bitten, long-established, professional marketeers.

In some cases, despite the youthful sales manager's meager practical background in commercial life, he applies his education, is intelligent enough to develop on the job and, eventually, justifies his appointment to responsibility. Occasionally, one comes to the fore whose early advancement to the company's top position, deludes him into thinking himself already a big man. I once had the misfortune to be saddled with such a sales manager, one who acted as though his accelerated growth with the company had increased his stature to ten feet tall.

Upon the occasion of a trip into our territory, this embryonic basketball player announced he particularly wanted to see a certain California distributor whose interest I had been nursing along in the faint hope he would take on our line. The oft-postponed decision was hanging dubiously on the difficult problems and debatable value of having to replace a heavily-stocked, long-handled competitor's line. It didn't look promising.

"I'll show you how to sell this guy," was my brash sales

manager's abrupt pronouncement as we discussed the prospect. "Let's go see him!" Blinking at this superb display of confidence, and somewhat wistfully wondering if I would care to be that youthful again, I thought it best to just murmur something about having been at it for quite a while but that I was always willing to learn.

I phoned the distributor to make an appointment. He apologized; too busy to accompany us for lunch, that in fact he had been "brown bagging it" but, if we wanted to stop by, as a matter of courtesy to my Eastern visitor, he would try to spare a few minutes just to meet him.

While en route to the distributor's place of business, I got the benefit of quotations from my sales manager's erstwhile business training course anent the necessity for making up a prospect's mind for him. He was still holding forth on my lack of aggressiveness, with unrestrained aspersions about the slowing-up effect of age, when we arrived at our destination. The introductory amenities scarcely over with, and blandly disregarding the distributor's hints that he had urgent matters requiring immediate attention, my ten-footer plunged right into a sales pitch. It culminated with him saying,

"If you don't buy the products we manufacture in the East, how do you expect us to buy your California oranges?"

The distributor's jaw tightened. He opened a desk drawer, took out his "brown bag" and said acidly, "I don't sell oranges." He withdrew an orange from the bag. "But here's one you can have for free. Now I don't have to buy your products. Good day!"

It was a long time before that distributor even allowed me to call on him again. Sadly contemplating the rubble of what had once been a good relationship, I vowed that, come hell or high water, if I were ever again similarly afflicted with one blown up by delusions of grandeur, I would cut him down to size before allowing him the opportunity of destroying my hard-earned standing with the trade.

But regardless of one's feelings, trying to "handle" your

sales manager can be a pretty dubious proposition. All too human failings on both sides can be manifested but, as a rule, it is the sales manager who has the last word. There can be a confrontation in a given situation wherein a determined rep, deeply disapproving the factory's course, comes up against the unyielding sales manager – and you are in deep trouble. You don't have much choice: persuasive powers failing, give in or give up the line. Fortunately, we don't often encounter such stupes as I have just described but, about in the same category, you may be saddled with one who, though perhaps well qualified in other ways, can break you with his line because sales managership just simply isn't his dish.

I recall a minor but ironical incident of an excellent engineer promoted to sales managership of his company. His background became immediately evident. He designed and introduced greatly needed standardization of packaging, accompanied with the ironclad rule that orders would be accepted only in standard cartons. He meant it. An order from one of our best customers, for 5,025 pieces of a quite high-priced goodie, packaged in units of 50, was promptly rejected. It was actually returned to the customer with a curt note, to either reduce the order to 5,000 or increase it to 5,050 . . . . It wasn't too long before he was back where he belonged, doing a fine job as a design engineer. (His replacement announced the standardized packaging would certainly be retained, but that an extra charge would apply to broken package orders. So simple! So commonplace! But our engineer just couldn't countenance such an unorthodox violation of his training.)

So what else makes a "good" sales manager from the rep's point of view? What about the one who irritates the rep by needling calls for more business? Well – just how bad is that? Though entirely cognizant of your ability, your obvious desire and need to turn in more orders, he is aware that, as human beings, there are times when we let down, that we are apt to lapse into discouragement when the going gets rough. Maybe it isn't so terrible as all that to be prodded a bit, once in a while, to spur on flagging efforts.

But, and this is where the understanding of human nature once again becomes so important: the "good" sales manager will know how and when to push. He will use judgment, tact, perhaps offer the carrot of special rewards for extra effort. He is the direct antithesis of the one who brandishes the knife of possible termination in the rep's face, who believes the way to manage men is to beat them over the head, who would be better termed a flails manager than a sales manager. How do you react to the bully?

It is difficult indeed to come up with an antidote that will counteract such a poisonality. When thus confronted, you will have to make a choice between one of two possible courses. First, consider this: back in the days when a preacher would roar out vivid, terrifying prophecies of the transgressor's afterlife, of Hell's flames perpetually dooming mankind's sinners, some listeners remained skeptical. They reasoned it was fallacious to believe in a Hell inflicting everlasting punishment, because people can get used to *anything*.

So, if you happen to become afflicted with one of those whip-cracking sales managers, a psychotic carried away with a headswimming sense of power, just look upon the relationship as an exercise in self-discipline. After all, if the line isn't too valuable, it is always possible to tell the dictatorial one you've removed the line's hooks so that he can shove it more easily. On the other hand, if the line is profitable, restrain your desire to punch the sonofabitch in the nose, reflect that dictators come and go, and cry your way to the bank. Because, if you don't know of a better world, you'll just have to make do with this one.

32
THE QUOTA

– a blessing in disguise

The rep may look upon market forecasting with reluctance, even a certain amount of resentment, when it leads to a specific quota imposed upon him by the manufacturer. He sniffs. Isn't he in business for himself? Doesn't that mean he *has* to give it all he's got, to extract every bit of business possible from the territory? He grumbles: why this superfluous, irritating pushing, this setting up of artificial goals?

Sorry, friend – you're going to have to get with it.

Market surveys and forecasting sales volume have become commonplace procedures whether the rep likes it or not. And experience has proved that a quota projection does have advantages, that the results can prove beneficial to the rep, *providing* it is an intelligently contrived figure.

We're all human. Sometimes monotony gets us down. A good quota, one stemming from close study of the individual territory, can act as a desirable spur. Instead of a vague, wishful desire to be doing more business, the rep becomes motivated by enforced concentration on a specific target. With that goal before him, he is likely to use a carefully aimed rifle rather than the scattered shotgun approach. The results are bound to be beneficial.

Unfortunately, one is occasionally confronted with the unthinking sales manager who imposes arbitrary quotas on his reps produced by short-sighted reasoning. A common misjudgment is when a sales manager cites national percentages which break down the country's territories by percent of sales volume. He claims that if territory A produces 10% of the country's business and territory B does 15%, his rep should come through with volume directly comparable in each territory.

To begin with, the usual national percentage figures vary all over the map. One has only to compare the computations of, say, manufacturing groups with government figures or those of respected trade publications, to see how they differ. It would be highly desirable to have a standardized, authoritative source for such tabulations but, in the past, such has not been the case.

The fallacy in this sales manager's reasoning is that he doesn't give enough consideration to the individual factors which differentiate a given territory from others. Local conditions will strongly influence business one way or another. A "good quota" first has to be based on actual past and current figures. (This is one place where that "Sales Volume Record," previously described, can be so helpful). It should allow for the state of the local market, what competition is doing, the bearing of national conditions, the possible changes in the trade's usage of the subject products. At its best, it would be a figure the sales manager arrives at by enlisting the aid of the rep.

One very practical approach used by cooperation (usually enforced!) starts with the rep being asked to compile a list of the territory's customers, to show each one's past volume coupled with the projected estimate of the following year's purchases. It is assumed, and rightfully, that the rep's intimate knowledge of what goes on with each customer far exceeds the sales manager's ability to guess at what may be expected in the future from a given set of customers.

True, such a compilation takes time and much concentrated thought. The projections can be no more than educated guessing. But, the finalized total establishes something approaching a realistic figure that can be reasonably used in setting up the quota. Of course, the smart manager knows the rep is going to be very conservative in the figure he submits because, he realizes, when the year is over, he can expect to be held to an accounting. If he doesn't reach the total, he may be taken to task. If he exceeds it, he has made himself look like a hero. But on the other hand, neither will he turn in figures *too* low, because that would make him look bad with the factory, So, albeit with a grain of tolerance, the sales manager will probably combine it with his own ideas and will make the quota higher than the rep's compilations. Nevertheless, such a *mutual* approach makes sense. It is to the rep's benefit to encourage and support that kind of working together.

For those seeking something more dependable than varying human calculations, the profound advantages of automation are now available for establishing quotas and long-range planning. In one case, offered by a company whose name is a national by-word, a modern day service consists of extensive quarterly reports detailing the country's economics, trends and so on. This is not at all the usual "letter service" guesstimating what is going to happen in the stock market and all that, but is a coldly impersonalized readout from the computer, data and trends scientifically compiled by automated processes – in short, a means for reducing the vagaries of estimates and opinions to facts.

In addition to national figures, the subscriber can feed raw data to the computer, based on his individual calculations and assumptions, by way of tailoring the desired information precisely to his own conditions. The cost to the subscriber is on the order of three or four hundred dollars per year. Considering the value dependable data offers for the increasing importance of forecasting market conditions, the rep could very well recommend and urge his principals to use such a service.

Sometimes fate hangs on to us a sales manager who

completely disregards good trade practice and common sense. He simply announces a quota for the coming year, a capricious figure, supported by nothing in rhyme or reason. Thankfully, there aren't too many such any more but, occasionally, one like that still comes along. He is apt to be the kind of hellion who enjoys cracking the whip over the helpless rep, an egotist who threatens with the quota as an adjunct of his sadistic instincts. The rep has little recourse if he is afflicted with such a character other than to react as he would to any person mentally disturbed.

Which brings to mind the rep who, after taking over a so-so line, by intensive promotion in two years tripled the manufacturer's previous sales volume. That achievement was followed one day by an amazing letter from the sales manager. It stated shortly that the rep's quota for the coming year was to be one-third over that of the previous year. Whereupon the rep responded with the following letter:

"I was very happy to learn about the increase expected in my income of one-third on your line over that of the past year. I appreciate your generosity very much because I can certainly use the money. But please satisfy my curiosity by explaining what you are going to do by way of accomplishing this pleasant surprise."

Which was the end of any more talk about absurd quotas for that line.

33
BIG VS. SMALL CUSTOMERS

Is there a preference?

You can have yourself a first class argument debating whether to concentrate on customers big enough to place proportionately large orders or to divide your time up among the smaller possibilities. Both sides of the question have their compelling points and their negative sides.

The frequently-heard remark that it doesn't take any longer to pick up a big order than a small one isn't very thoughtful, when applied to the big customers. Start with this situation: consider how many reps, both independent and direct factory men, are in business in your territory. Practically every one of them is shooting at the big accounts. You have tremendous competition, not only for the buyer's time, but from the multitude of choices for selecting his purchases. You and your wares are just one of a big conglomeration, awaiting the buyer's attention. You have to call repeatedly, before you can get just that first interview.

With a large company, the likelihood for frustrations are many. For instance, suppose you've waited it out, worked your way in and are now finally dealing with the cognizant buyer. Having gone through all the sweat of presenting your pitch, struggling through several calls, you are told various people concerned had yet to approve, but it looks good. Then comes that miserable "turnover" of help for which the electronic industry in particular is noted.

You come in about the time you should be picking up your order, only to find your man has been transferred to another department or resigned to take a job elsewhere. You are now confronted with a new buyer, who knows nothing about the deal, who puts you off until he can "catch up with what's going on." You have to start your pitch from scratch, all over again, with the samples, with the quotations, and all the rest.

That example, of course, is only a possibility – unfortunately, it occurs all too often. Then, too, you are aware that your "big" company buyer is a busy, harassed man. While trying to hold his time and undivided attention, subconsciously your recollection of that mob in the reception room waiting to get at him, forces a hurried, perhaps disorderly presentation, as you try to put your points over. It does not make for a good interview.

Yup, indeed it do take a long, hard time to "pick up" (!) a big order.

How about the smaller accounts? Sure, there's the credit problem – but, that's part of the game .... It's easier and faster to get to the one or two key men. Not being over-run with reps, they can give you more time, are more receptive to your story. Decisions are apt to come quicker. Their orders may (or may not!) be smaller but, the length of time it takes to get them may amount to no more than waiting to be interviewed by the big boys and could produce as much commission in the aggregate – maybe more.

Getting "in" when they are small establishes you with an inside track as they grow. Small accounts are likely to be more appreciative of your services than the larger, blase accounts. Your dealings are closer to that "final say" (i.e., "management," perhaps the owner himself), thereby considerably speeding things up.

Many reps "just haven't the time" to call on small accounts – perhaps because they are using it up, sitting around in reception offices, waiting to talk to the big shot buyers?

I suppose, in the final analysis, it comes down to a

question of manpower. You should cover all bases but, naturally, you want to get the most return within the limitations of your selling time. Those big, fat orders, with no credit problems, are very alluring. But are they always "big" and "fat"? Does the *size* of the company *necessarily* mean the orders will be proportionately large?

An expeditious approach to the small account is simple enough. You have only to regularly go over the bingo cards and other leads you may have received about new possibilities, and call them on the phone. You can get a pretty good idea right then and there of how much further you should go. If it sounds favorable, you make your appointments – a quick, economical process that will get you right down to brass tacks with a minimum of effort.

In this rapid-fire, technological world, the small customer of today has a way of becoming tomorrow's big account. How nice it is! to be one of the favored among those who grow with him.

34
PUBLICITY

National advertising for free

"I don't care what they call me, so long as they spell my name right." That corny joke stems from a profound realization of publicity's value. Surely, undue modesty is hardly a feature of the kind of man who essays to become a manufacturers' representative. So why most reps overlook this self-evident tool for helping establish that all-important image, in places where it counts – and for free – well, it just beats me!

Of the various national publications devoted to industry, many welcome news concerning doings in the trade. Items about rep firms are published about moving into new, expanded quarters, of the growth indicated by the announcement of a new man to the staff, of celebrating an extended number of years in business, of plaques awarded for a distinctive achievement, of appointment to some trade committee, of taking on a new line, and so on. If not hair-raising, to business readers such minor events are, nevertheless, of interest.

Public relations? Simply a euphemism for advertising. And haven't you noticed how many multi-million-dollar campaigns are aimed at no more than establishing familiarity with the advertiser's *name*? It comes under the heading of "creating an image."

There is no reason why you, too, shouldn't try to establish so-called "subliminal" impressions of your firm, particularly since it costs you nothing. It's in your interests, one facet of building a reputation for yourself. For instance: a sales manager, considering applications for his line, recognizes something vaguely familiar about your firm name. He's "heard it somewhere" but probably just can't recall where – something or other about your activities – and immediately your application stands out. As a matter of fact, it is likely that his recognition could have stemmed solely from some one or two items he happened to read about you in the past while skimming through some of the trade magazines.

At a convention in New York, a rep with whom I had the same line in common, was talking about this very point, and how assiduously he issued "p.r." about himself. It led to a story of how he acquired the line. One day he received a long distance call from an old friend with whom he had long lost touch. "I hear you've become a high-powered rep," the caller said. "Can you use a good line?" It developed that he was the manufacturer of a series of products fitting perfectly into the rep's picture. A sales arrangement was soon made, to work out profitably for all concerned.

"I just met the guy who recommended me for the line," he chuckled. "I had never met him before – I understand he reps the line somewhere in the South. But he knew me. 'I read about you all the time!' he said. 'You're always active – must be doing a big job out there. That's how come, when I heard the sales manager saying he needed a rep in your territory, I suggested your name.' "

"I'm taking the guy out to a steak dinner tonight," my friend grinned. "Guess that's about the least I can do!"

By way of coining a phrase – it pays to advertise.

35
ETHICS; LAW OF THE JUNGLE

– and termination clauses

Some years ago, a distributor friend of mine spent his vacations poking around in ghost towns, being especially intrigued by the implications and histories engraved on time-worn, crumbling headstones in the old graveyards. While telling me of experiences during a trip from which he had recently returned, he quoted an inscription from one of these monuments:

> "Here lies the body of a gal named Maginity.
> For thirty years she retained her virginity.
> A damn good record for this vicinity."

It's a jingle that brings to mind my initial experience with an attempted violation of my unsullied being. This happened in my very first year in the rep business. A certain rep had tried to molest me by inveigling an order from a customer intended for one of my factories. I learned his evil intention was to use it as evidence that I wasn't taking care of the customers, in his attempts to wean the line away from me.

The line was averaging me a hundred bucks a month, just the amount delegated to taking care of my car payments. Still virginly naive about these things and panicky over the prospect of losing my car, I variously envisioned punching the dastardly creature in the nose, begging the sales manager not to terminate me, all the way to suing the guy on the grounds of illegal piracy. Just at that moment, however, I acquired two new lines and, my attention happily diverted, did nothing about the unscrupulous wretch's wicked intentions.

He didn't get anywhere. I had been doubling the business done by the rep who had given the line up before I came aboard and the factory was entirely happy with my services. (In fact, when I retired fifteen years later, I still had the same line.)

What a controversial word is "ethics," with its explosive potential lending itself to varying interpretations. It's like the word, "obscenity." Everyone knows what it is, but how do you define it? Nevertheless, "ethics" looms up big in relationships between fellow reps and their respective principals.

An unfortunate aspect of repping, is the lack of security written into sales agreements. Sales contracts are drawn up presumably covering every contingency. Both parties are in full accord. But somewhere tucked into the jargon is sure to appear a sentence which, no matter how tactfully worded, makes it very clear that the rep's services may be terminated at the principal's discretion, with or without cause. That the rep has the same privilege by way of right to resign the line, that some improvements are being made in extending the ridiculously short "30-day termination" clauses, does not gainsay the fact that the principal is at all times in the saddle.

So what has that to do with ethics? Simply that the rep is vulnerable. It is within any whimsy of the sales manager that the rep may or may not be fired. Which, in turn, provides the opening for the predatory type of rep to sneak in.

The newcomer to the business may in all innocence transgress the boundaries of professional ethics. In one sense, in cold-blooded language, *any* line can be considered "up for grabs." The tyro may, with a certain amount of self-justification, stand on the legal principle that he has just as much right as anybody else to compete in this world of economics. If he can establish in a principal's mind the belief that he can do better with that line than the existing rep, why shouldn't he make a try for it? What's so dirty about that?

Well, assume the case of an architect or a building contractor. He is entitled to bid in open competition for a job but, once the contract has been let, does he try to take it away from the winning competitor? Do lawyers and doctors attempt to swipe trade from each other? *You* wouldn't knowingly patronize the man who violates the recognized ethics of his calling; you'd be afraid of him, wouldn't you? The better sales manager is likely to exhibit the same skepticism when approached by one attempting to breach his contractual relationship with another rep. Evidence of trade scruples lacking in an aspirant is one of the best protections for the rep who already has the line. But, pragmatically speaking and over all, as in the case of my initial experience, if you're doing a good job, the other guy is going to play hell trying to get it away from you.

In any event, regardless of high-minded sales managers and multi-page contracts, no *definitive* protection from the unethical one exists. Which brings up the corollary that, in turn, *neither is the man safeguarded* who gets a line away unfairly from another rep. He invites retaliation. The matter of respecting the other fellow's rights, whether implied or otherwise becomes then, per se, important for self-protection. Otherwise the law of the jungle would prevail. And the good Lord knows, a rep has enough problems of survival without having to worry about the prospects of being attacked by a fellow rep. Nevertheless, we do occasionally encounter one who disregards the consequences of his business practices.

Ordinarily, the unscrupulous rep doesn't openly, blatantly tackle his objective. He'll usually follow a circuitous route, though there are innumerable variations. One common example should suffice: the scene, a convention, where a certain rep got himself introduced to the manager of a well-known line. The sales manager asked politely, "How's business out your way?" The rep said it was good but he needed one more line. "If I could only pick up a line like yours," he threw out off-handedly. He began to speak of how qualified he was to handle such lines. Quickly sensing the direction of the rep's words, the sales manager broke in with "We've had Jack X . . . . representing us in your territory for a number of years. You know him?"

"Jack X . . . .?" responded the rep. "You mean to tell me – with all his money, he's still repping? Gosh, I haven't seen him around on the territory in ages. He's a great golfer, you know – always out there winning cups and things."

"Yes," said the frowning sales manager shortly, "I know," and abruptly turned away. A veteran of the business, he understood only too well the crude attempt to plant the thought that his rep was neglecting his work. (It so happened that the next time he made a field trip into his rep's territory, the two of them spent a Saturday afternoon on the golf course, where he was reminded of the incident. They both chuckled over it, although the story didn't help the rep's game any!)

Naturally, if a line is known to be "open," any rep is privileged to go after it. But there is no excuse for even the veriest tyro remaining in ignorance of whether a line is or is not already represented before throwing his pitch for it. Reps and their lines are commonly listed in trade directories. A judicious enquiry or two among customers or fellow reps can elicit the information. If one has heard a rumor that a certain rep agreement has been terminated, he can contact the referenced rep to verify the story. For the conscientious rep, it isn't all that difficult. He may ask, where can a high-minded, self-respecting newcomer find a "do and don't" code for guiding one's conduct properly in the rep business? Well, there is such a code of ethics – long established, quite simple and easy to understand. It's known as THE GOLDEN RULE. Like, if you would DO AS YOU WOULD BE DONE BY, no one can ask for anything more!

36
CUSTOMER CREDIT

The rep makes like D & B

Some reps shrug off responsibility of any kind for payment of the customers' obligations to the principal. After all, the manufacturer has to have a Credit Manager back there upon whom such duties devolve – that's his job, not the rep's.

Nevertheless, the principal does have a right to look to his rep for help in credit matters. In some cases, he relies entirely upon the rep to steer him right. The fact that the rep has no legal responsibility in such matters does not gainsay the moral implications of his position.

Assume an order being taken from a new account. The principal is far away, knows nothing of this customer. He must rely on commercial credit agencies and/or his rep. In many cases, because of being right there, probably personally acquainted with the customer, the rep has more intimate knowledge of the financial practices and status of the account than do the national agencies. It is up to him to advise the factory accordingly.

If previously unfamiliar with the account, the rep need have no hesitancy, – in fact he *should* ask for financial statements, for credit references. Why not? Let the new customer realize that *you* have responsibility in this matter, that *all* concerned have to be assured the order will be paid for. And if the customer is evasive or declines to supply satisfactory information, you can take this as a red flag signal; you'd better right then and there mark the order C.O.D. or refuse to take it.

A surprising fact is that many reps fail to take advantage

of a simple, quick way to get good information about a customer's financial responsibility from a knowledgeable, neutral source. You have only to contact his bank. Talk with one of the officers. He'll give you a good idea of how much money the customer has on deposit, ("his balance runs in the low five figures"), how long they have had the account, whether or not they have had satisfactory credit dealings with him and how much of a line of credit they are willing to extend him.

Sometimes by mail, but I used to get this presumably confidential information in most cases right over the phone, just by making a brief explanation of who I was and why I was calling. Only once did a bank official refuse to tell me what I wanted to know. In that case, I called my own bank, who got the desired information for me promptly.

If a customer becomes delinquent in paying his account, the rep is apprised of the fact by copies of statements and dunning letters. Though perhaps unpleasant, it is *his* duty to somehow get into the act, to help his principal collect.

It is common that a customer may remain totally oblivious to the distant manufacturer's importunities for payment, but just let him get a call from the local rep and his check comes forth. Why?

It's hard to say. Very often the customer doesn't realize the rep is aware of his delinquency, relying upon the assumption that the rep isn't supposed to be concerned with collections. It embarrasses him to learn what the situation really is and he hastens to rectify it. Another explanation is the personal touch – it always beats even a strongly worded but lifeless piece of paper (especially if it is recognizable as a form letter). But he does come through.

Of course, you have to keep this in mind: *anyone* functioning even temporarily in the guise of a credit man can collect, assuming the account has the necessary assets, but it takes a *good* credit man to make the collection and *keep the customer, too*!

Anyway – the rep as a bill collector works, and since a manufacturer's representative truly represents the factory and all its interests in his territory, it is manifestly his duty to see that the factory gets paid for the orders he produced.

And as a footnote to the foregoing, it has to be acknowledged that there are still some horse-and-buggy, small-thinking manufacturers who don't pay *commissions* until the *customer* pays *them*. If it is your lot to be repping for such a manufacturer, it obviously certainly behooves you to get on the ball and see that the accounts pay up.

37
THE REP AS A DISTRIBUTOR

How do you divide one by two?

No matter what dodge or evasion a rep uses (*if* he is so minded), it is nevertheless fact that under whatever conditions a rep stocks merchandise in premises under his control, when he ships and bills, he is a *distributor*. Which is not to imply any wrong-doing by engaging in such a business. Quite the contrary! Today, such forms of enterprise are popularly commonplace, often highly profitable. For some reps, it is also a good way to lose their shirts. Make no mistake about it, repping and distributing are two, very distinctly different kinds of operations, best kept apart.

Every rep thinks of stocking at some point in his career. Maybe his considerations are prompted by the character and conditions having to do with only one line. More often, he is bugged by the anomaly that both he and the "regular" distributor call on the same buyer – but on the resultant order, the distributor makes twenty-some-odd to forty percent,while the rep makes only a measly fraction thereof. If a rep's thinking remains that shallow and he proceeds on such assumption, he's in for a rude awakening.

There have been some spectacular outcomes of reps turning to the distributor business. One well-known rep comes to mind who built up an operation employing over forty persons. In another case, a group of reps formed a nation-wide chain of distribution, each rep in his territory serving the requirements of the area, to result in an operation doing many millions of dollars worth of business per year. Numerous successful instances can be cited of at least partial distribution enterprises entered into by reps. Given due consideration of the capital and "know-how" required and the inherent risks, some form of "distribution" holds promising possibilities for the rep.

A not uncommon instance of how one rep was drawn somewhat inadvertently into the distribution business came about because of his lack of success in selling any distributors in his territory a line of considerable quality and price merit. The product was in a very competitive category. All the usual distributors stocked two or three similar and well-known lines – they could see no point in multiplying their inventories with still another such line.

Disgruntled by his inability to establish even one distributor, this rep turned to stocking the line himself. Fearful of the possible consequences, for a while he took the trouble to explain, to meet charges of competing with his own customers by pointing to the fact that the dealer trade was willing to buy his product if it were locally stocked, but that every distributor had passed up the chance to handle it. In the course of time, he discontinued bothering to make such excuses.

He did very well for himself. The thorough job he performed of establishing the line, led him into stocking other compatible lines; within a few years, he built up a business employing twenty people. Though continuing his rep business, he found the profits of distribution outweighed the commission checks he received as a rep. Of course, he became persona non grata as a rep to the regular distributor trade. It didn't worry him because he was now a full-fledged distributor himself, openly competing with the regulars. About his dwindling rep business, he couldn't care less. But they don't all turn out that way.

Where many reps fall on their faces when it comes to stocking lines is not realizing the differences between being a manufacturers' representative and "keeping store." The deceptively large, gross discount offered distributors is exactly that – *gross*. By the time the distributor has paid for rent, freight, staff of inside and outside employees, insurance, bookkeeping, credit losses, mysterious inventory shrinkage, catalogs, interest on loans, obsolete stock, advertising, taxes and a thousand and one other expense items, his net profit on the huge investment required can very well shrink to less than the return on an ordinary rep operation, to say nothing of the headaches accompanying a multi-detailed merchandising business. Under today's conditions, it takes a mighty well managed distributor operation to net 6% to 8% whereas 2% is closer to what all too many have left over for themselves when the year is over.

Some reps stock merchandise not to compete with their customers but, rather, to offer convenient, fast delivery to the "regular" distributors (sometimes with a small surcharge added). This would seem reasonable enough, as rendering an extra service to one's customers. But even to this limited degree, don't forget that it is going to cost you. It ties up some of your capital. There's your time to think about in acting as a shipping department, much more paper work, the vicissitudes of inventorying, of keeping track of what is "in," what is "coming in," what has "gone out," to whom and when; the responsibility factor, necessitating frequent reports to the factory, plus fire and burglary insurance; special applicable licenses and taxes. Not the least to contend with is the customer who pleads for or demands instant delivery, knowing you have the stock, at a time when you are immersed in other work.

Or, if you are going to sell the kind of trade whom the distributor considers his customer, are you prepared to risk the onus of being regarded as a competitor? Can you look with equanimity upon the necessity for making a choice between manufacturers' representation and distribution? Because, straddling two horses with only one pair of legs is quite a trick!

Which way to go or stay can come pretty close to calling for a coin-flipping decision. There is certainly nothing wrong about remaining strictly a manufacturers' representative in the traditional sense, handling no more than an occasional sample when it comes to the merchandise. It is a rewarding profession in itself. But as one means of expansion, the transition from repping into distributing, though fraught with hazards, holds profitable possibilities.

Just one word more: among the many pro and con factors, one thing in particular might weigh up heavily; the distributor can point to the visible, physical evidence of an established, salable business, with substantial, tangible assets, such as inventory, accounts receivable and so on. In the final analysis, the rep's business is embodied entirely in him, himself. *He* is the business.

But isn't that why he chose to become a rep in the first place?

38
THE HIRING SALESMEN PROBLEM

What price "associate?"

"Good salesmen are hard to get."

Not exactly news, eh? But just why is the problem so commonplace that we make a cliche out of the expression?

The usual difficulties of hiring the right kind of man are painfully familiar. And as long as you go at it in the usual way, offering the usual kind of job, you can expect continuance of the usual help problems. Like: you'd like to hire a man who has selling experience, attractive personality, product knowledge, enthusiasm, familiarity with trade personnel, willingness to work hard and a few other little qualifications like that there. One might say, a man practically like yourself – right? But if a man has all those attributes, you might ask yourself, what does he need *you* for? Can't he just as well go out on his own, same as you did?. . . . No, a paragon like that isn't interested in just a job.

When it comes to needing help, it is probably the growing "one-man" operation who is in the toughest spot. His income doesn't provide enough to pay a salesman adequately. He can't afford to "carry" him for the length of time it takes a man to become a producer. It *could* be built up to that point, but how? On whose money? Because of his circumstances, the best the rep can offer is just a straight commission deal, some kind of split with the prospective salesman. He might pay for expenses.

It rarely works. Assume the man accepts the offer. He

puts in hard, long hours. He tries. But – no matter how good his potential, it takes a long time to learn the fine points of all the lines. If, as and when he starts possible deals, the necessity for repeated calls back, the time it takes to finally pick up and fill orders, followed by the long wait for the commission checks to come through, all add up to months and months. Meanwhile, where is the money coming from to meet his rent or mortgage payments, food for his family, car payments, etc., etc.? How *can* a deal like this work out favorably for the salesman?

After a few fiascos and, especially, tiring of snide remarks from customers about his frequent turnover of help, the rep usually winds up by resignedly working his head off, until he has built up enough income to offer a prospective salesman adequate compensation. So – then what?

I wish the word "empathy" were in more common use. The very mental process of using it frequently induces trying to think like the other fellow – putting yourself in his shoes. I am almost tempted to define it as mind-reading. Anyway – let's assume you have before you a man who looks like the kind of salesman you want. So what do you suppose is going on in *his* mind. Oh? You think so? Is it really *only* money?

You offer a likely looking applicant a guarantee, plus some kind of percentage on sales, and expenses – perhaps even adding a form of profit-sharing. Sound fair enough? Well – think back to when you started. Didn't you, yourself, pass up such "just a job" kind of propositions, even though they might have paid reasonably well? Didn't you choose to struggle in the rep business, for the chance to create something better for yourself than simply being an employee of somebody else? Maybe this applicant, too, is thinking of something beyond "just a pretty good job." Could he be seeking an opportunity to supplant *you*?

Okay – maybe, in this instance, you're looking at a fellow who *is* only interested in the immediate paycheck;

usually, that is the situation. He seems to be fairly well qualified. You agree on terms and hire him. He does well enough. Maybe he stays with you; perhaps leaves for the first attractive offer a competitor makes. Or, he goes along; for lack of better, you keep this mediocrity on the payroll, satisfied to have a good workhorse around. And, for the time being, that's that. You sigh, "life is a series of compromises."

But what about the *exceptional* man? Suppose an applicant comes along full of you-know-what plus vinegar? He's ambitious, alert; in addition to the usual qualifications, he's obviously intelligent, well poised, self-confident. He asks *you* searching questions – about the personalities of your principals, how much business you're doing and other more-or-less proprietary matters. One would think he contemplates hiring *you*!

Confronted with such an outstanding man, the average rep turns pale. He shies away and gets rid of the guy soon as possible. Dynamite! he tells himself. This character will stick around just long enough to accumulate a nest egg. He'll cozy up to my principals and next thing that happens, he'll leave and take a couple of my lines with him. No – sir! Not him!

Well, now, wait a minute. Maybe. And then again – maybe not. That man may be the very heaven-sent guy you *should* latch onto – *providing* you're looking far ahead, considering that *some* day, you're going to need somebody to take over your place when you're ready to retire. If that man has sufficient potential for making it on his own, he not only can make a major contribution to building up your business but, when the time comes for you to get out, you could have a ready-made buyer available (and I don't have to tell you, buyers for a rep business are kinda hard to come by!)

Such a man, having the wherewithal to be a successful rep, will have sufficient ken to realize how long and hard is the road. Maybe – he's thinking – there's an easier way. That way, aside from immediate financial remuneration, is probably occupying his mind.

The process of eliminating the hopeless applicants is one, of course, which you can't escape. And, being human, you might make one or two mistaken selections. Only time can tell. But suppose, ultimately, the trial period over, you have before you a highly desirable man, one capable of becoming an "associate" in the true meaning of the word. What does it take to hold him? Do you have to give up an arm and a leg? Well – maybe, at least an arm. Which is to say: you've got to proffer more than "just a job." In short, *you've got to put him in business for himself* – in *your* business. It's up to you to present a proposition whereby at some pre-determined future time, *he* will own a substantial portion, if not *all* of your business.

Yup. It is, indeed, hard to do. Nobody did it for you. Every one of us, wrestling with the necessity for *giving* a man ownership in the business, thinks back over his years of sacrifice, of hard work. You bemoan the conditions that make it necessary to ease the way for the Johnny-come-lately employee, how you have to provide him with a living income right off the reel, with ownership in an established business, something nobody did for *you*. Why should you hand over what you built yourself to some other guy, just like that?

Because, like it or not – just like that is the way the economic structure of this country is built. After one has put in the foundation, set up the framework, help is now needed to get on with the job. You can't do it alone. So, you've got to pay for that help. It can be done by struggling along with day-to-day labor or, if you're planning for the future, by sooner or later giving him a piece of the action.

It is pretty well established that the process of bringing up a salesman to the point where his services are profitable to the business, can cost the employer many thousands of dollars, some placing the figure up to $30,000. If the rep employer is going to have to come up with that kind of money out of his own pocket, to gamble on a man who may leave just as he is beginning to be worth his salt, maybe it is smarter to devise a way of giving that salesman the means he needs, in one form or another, to buy his way into the business, thereby locking him in. How much are you really sacrificing if you compensate him with stock (i.e., ownership) in your company? What I am getting at – by-passing the details for the time being – is that, by giving up part of your ownership (a) the business acquires a man who will stay with it, and who will help build that business, who will work as loyally, as hard and conscientiously as you do because *he's working for himself* and (b) you establish a feasible situation that will ease the problem of retiring from the business when that day comes.

What all this boils down to is you have two approaches to the problem of hiring salesman: one is to look upon the man as temporary – that is, though he may be around even for years, his status is never more than that of an employee, with his termination possible at most any time for any one of a number of reasons. That is no solution for what is to be a steadily recurring problem. The other way is, you acquire an "associate" – a man to work *with* you, not just for you, and who becomes a part of the ownership, along with you.

But of course, you can always elect to remain a one-man operation.

This subject will come up again in the chapter headed "Anticipating Retirement."

39
YOUR WEAK SPOTS

A way of self-analysis

Seeking out the weaknesses of your operation may be compared to a surgeon probing his own body. For example: few problems confronting the rep are quite as frustrating as trying to analyze whether a given line should be kept or dropped.

An outside consultant called in, to be armed with all the applicable figures and facts, might be helpful – perhaps, say, your accountant? It's a tough one. One approach to the answer is to *write out* those "applicable facts and figures" in complete detail, just as though *actually* intended for this outsider. (Do *not* dictate it to your secretary. That would defeat the whole idea. You must write it out *yourself*.) Set out the favorable and the adverse in side by side columns for easy *visual* comparison.

What does this accomplish? There is something about the compulsion of having to pin down, to transform one's thoughts into *exact written out words*, that brings into play a process of the mind tending to straighten out thinking, to help arrive at a conclusion. It is not too different from resorting to the blackboard before others when working out a problem in mathematics. In spelling it out on paper, as though in order to make the situation clearly understandable to someone else, one sets up a mental procedure that *compels* organizing thoughts in logical progression, thus leading to a conclusion.

If there is no time urgency, an extension of the same procedure is to lay aside your written description of the situation long enough to let it get cold. At some later date, you pick it up and re-read it. You now come at it almost like that outsider, with a fresh approach. You might discover contradictions, perhaps omissions of important facts which have bearing on the problem. The more significant portions stand out. You could be led right into the solution you have been seeking.

Maybe it's just me, but I'm hepped on this process. It has frequently served me well. I most earnestly urge you to try it once or twice. What can you lose? And you may be surprised to learn what it can do for you.

There are those who, upon reading the foregoing, will dismiss it with a snorting, "Oh, hell – I can't write!" Isn't that a confession of inability to think clearly? The same man will insist that he "can talk" but – in writing?

Why not? He uses the language of the land, of his craft, doesn't he? Something like this doesn't call for literary skill. Grammar is immaterial. No, what his excuse boils down to is that when he *talks*, he can and does keep repeating himself over and over again, in order to make himself understood. But to write it out, he has to invoke self-discipline, to stop and *think* of just the right, applicable words in order to express himself. It's a process of *enforcing* oneself to channel thought in a straight line toward Q.E.D.

40
THE BRANCH OFFICE

How far does a rubber band stretch?

It is well known that a goodly number of reps across the country have prospered in branch operations, in some cases most spectacularly. Yet, one cannot help but wonder: with every territory continually developing a never-ceasing succession of new, prospective customers, why not cultivate one's own immediate surroundings rather than stretch into distant fields, with all the problems such expansion entails? There are innumerable single office establishments which, nevertheless, write multi-million-dollar business annually. In addition to regular representation, it is possible to enter into affiliated operations such as, perhaps, stocking merchandise, importing, and/or light manufacturing, thereby creating a big enterprise practically all under one roof. It has been done. This writer knows of one rep firm in particular, out of one establishment, in an area by no means among the so-called "big" territories of the country that, by such extension of activities, has grown to proportions large enough to employ something approaching a hundred persons.

In any case, for the rep who longingly contemplates the presumably lovely, lush fields of distant pastures, much thought should be given to the very real, choking weed growth he is likely to find if, as and when he starts plowing there. For instance, assuming the lines are available, of course securing the proper manpower becomes the first big problem. That has been the downfall of many reps who have tried to expand via the branch office route. Even though otherwise qualified, the man on whom one can rely to faithfully perform without on-the-spot supervision is rare, with inevitable come-and-go constant changes bedeviling the owner in need of good men.

The simply remarkable number of petty, contemptible methods distant, supposedly honest employees can manage to evolve for "cheating on the house" are beyond count. The routine by which a rep business is conducted ordinarily prevents the amounts of money so involved from being substantial. I have heard men shrug this off with a cynical, "part of the cost of doing business."

But the less forgiving must grit their teeth when confronted with dishonest practices, as they range through collecting for customer entertainment which never happened or by duplicating expense vouchers, phony gas and other auto maintenance bills, charging up dining out or traveling expenses to the company for their accompanying wives (or facsimiles thereof!), having their wives' personal cars maintained at company expense, purloining stamps and office supplies and the devil only knows how many more unique methods they can contrive for gnawing little holes in the ship.

And, of course, gold-bricking, taking time off from the job for outside personal activities, is always possible. Plus, of primary importance, the advantages of that personal face-to-face association with the customers by which you founded your business, are largely lost in branch operations.

Nevertheless, too many highly successful branch operations exist for anyone to condemn this kind of expansion. In the case of ERA's members, for example, of some 1,700 offices across the country, about 500 are branches.

As usual, circumstances alter cases.

41
IS IT BETTER TO BE BIGGER?

Small lines, big lines and nets

When it comes to building a bigger and better business –

And – not too common but conceivable – a line comes along where the commission checks read in four figures –

Assuming such an opportunity offers, no rep in his right mind is going to turn down that "big" line. Isn't that what you always say? That's what most reps would say.

But –

You might have second thoughts.

Much of the decision depends on why one chose to become a manufacturers' representative. Is it *mainly* for the money in it? I cannot support this with statistical proof but, judging reps as I have come to know them, I would say that in the long run, a goodly percentage have the qualifications to do better financially working for the other fellow – that is to say, some large corporation. So, prima-facie, it would seem that financial return, important though it may be, is not necessarily the primary reason why a man elects to become a rep.

So what is?

Well, as you will remember, we've said it many times before. *Independence*! Yup – the desire, the *need* to be your own boss!

So – what has this to do with the desirability of the "big" line? Just this – that when you take on the "big" line, you give up a large measure of that freedom from the corporate machine, the reason you chose to be a rep in the first place.

Aw right, let's face it: many a rep is quite willing to sacrifice his position as arbiter of his own fate when it comes to the possibility of acquiring a line that promises him two or three grand or so per month. And what's so bad about that? Why, nothing! Nothing at all! Except that –

You'll earn it! Every nickel of it!

You'll have to answer to several so-called "factory men" instead of just one sales manager, each of whom will have something imperative to say about how you handle your business. A line producing that kind of money, in most cases involves a large, multi-personnel corporation, with the rep subservient to a variety of authoritarian brass.

You'll be a captive, at the beck and call of the "factory men." Their communications become directives. Whether ready, willing or not, when one of them snaps his fingers, you'll have to jump. The "big" line will demand far more attention and service than your other lines, probably to the detriment of the latter. You'll have to pay out a goodly portion of that fat commission for more high-powered help than you would otherwise need – along with all the employee problems *that* entails.

And, you'll be beset by continual need for reports – endless paper work. When the factory calls for your presence, holding sales meetings at odd times, in remote places, you will have to be there, regardless of your other inclinations or duties. Because "big" lines have such apparent charms, you'll be a continual target for competitors. Large corporations are always susceptible to mergers, to being bought out by conglomerates, followed by cold-blooded kicking-out of existing reps. You'll be in sleep-disturbing jeopardy at all times, worrying about the possibility of losing such a major portion of your business by likelihood of the factory going "direct," and what that would do to you.

I know all this can be dismissed with a shrug, even a sneer. Many will say, Nuts! Just give me a chance to get hold of one of those big lines and watch how fast I'll grab it! Sure, there are objections, but I'll take my chances.

Okay – if that's how you feel about it. You've got lots of company. Nevertheless, I am going to express a contrary opinion, and you can take it for what it's worth – mainly, that the *ideal* rep roster may very well be a reasonable number of so-called "small" lines (for lack of better words, I mean those that pay up to a few hundred dollars a month).

You can be fairly comfortable with the small lines. In the normal course of events, factory "managements" are not going to be *too* demanding of you – they know you *can* get along without them; they can ask only so much of you. If you're turning in a reasonable amount of business, you're in good shape. There is none of the pressure which accompanies trying to get million-dollar deals because there are none such in the cards. And, they add up.

With the small line, you don't have to put on special help just because of that line, with the unpleasant consequence of having to fire good men when you lose it. If, as and when you terminate with a small line, you can tell yourself, So What! The loss is no tragedy.

If your lines are small, you retain your independence, your right to do things your own way within reason, even to telling that factory how *they* should be doing it. If your lines are small, you can always add one or two new ones, without having to go in for big expansion. If another line comes along, offering advantages over an existing line, you don't have to rebuild your entire business in order to make the switch. If you don't like the way the sales manager talks to you, it is no great loss for you to terminate *him*.

As a manufacturers' representative, you are in a personality business. But, in handling a "big" line, your personality becomes submerged. In effect, your position is that of a cog in the corporate machine; in which case, you might as well become a direct employee, with an assured income, and shed the responsibility devolving upon you when you are the head man.

In short: with "small" lines, you are in the saddle. With "big" lines you are the horse. To ride or be ridden, that is the question!

But let's consider another phase of "big" vs. "small" business, aside from individual lines per se. So far, we've naturally been going along with the usual desire of reps to increase the size of their operations, the assumption being that the bigger the sales volume, the more money one makes. All things being equal, presumably this is true. So you strive, you work hard, you knock yourself out, you employ help, you promote, you do everything in your power to build a bigger and better business.

You may do it. Many do.

But the key word in any business is PROFIT. Assume you are selling components. You can do a million dollars volume of sales at, say, 2% net profit, thereby making $20,000. Or, you can do only $400,000 but at 5% net, and make the same twenty grand. So?

Well, consider this: just being conservative, one man brings in the $400,000 worth of business. So what does it take to get up to $1 million? Would it be reasonable to say, the equivalent of two-and-a-half men? That is, one more salesman plus maybe another girl in the office and the miscellaneous increased expenses naturally entailed in handling the enlarged business? In which case, after it's all said and done – how much money is left for *you* when the year is over with? What's your net, net, net – your *profit*? More than $20,000?

I have deliberately generalized. The very basic figures cited will vary widely from one firm to another. I am only trying to plant this question in your mind – knowing that as business increases in size and correspondingly decreases in net percentage of profit, might it not be just as rewarding to stay small and make the bigger profit?

No, I'm not preaching or even suggesting a negative philosophy. If you are the kind of man who has the ambition and drive that draws one into the rep business, you're damned well going to be a fighter for bigger and better things and I'd be the last one to try and discourage you. I'm just allowing for the fact that, you're human. When you're unhappy about that "big" line that would have brought your business into the multi-million-dollar category, when you think you need more manpower to build a bigger business but can't afford to increase your payroll, there is consolation in the fact that what counts is how many *dollars* remain for just lil ole *you* after the year is over. Plus, you're still holding the reins in *your* hands.

42
COFFEE BREAK

Odds and ends to think about between sips

Here are a couple of gimmick ideas to kick around, for the rep who wants to get away from the ordinary. While not quite equal to taking off for the moon, such departures from the mundane help distinguish you from run-of-the-mill reps by presenting something a bit "different."

Knee of the Curve:

You commonly present price/quantity breakdowns to your customers in one form or another. You might try this twist: as a graphic means of submitting these figures, work up a curve, with the perpendicular labeled "price" and the horizontal base indicating "quantity." Start with the highest price for the smallest quantity: in projecting the curve, show the prices come down as the quantities increase.

Reproduce this curve. (If you think you will use a considerable number, it could be an inexpensive "instant printing" offset job; if only a few, knock them out on your copier.) Present a copy to the buyer with a prominent "X" marked at the "knee of the curve." That is: point out the amounts he normally buys, but with the "X" indicating somewhat larger quantities, by way of persuasive temptation to save money by ordering at the "X" break quantities.

The info request or appointment card:

Here's one for giving the conventional a light, "different"

touch. Have imprinted a quantity of postage-prepaid cards, addressed to you, to read something like this:

> Dear Joe (or whoever): Date................
> As an outside possibility – *some* day, we might just *possibly* have an order for you. No promises but, I'll think about it – *providing* you send me a catalog on
> ....
> quote me on ....
> show up at my desk on ....
>
> Name ....
>
> Company ....
>
> Address ....
>
> .... Phone ....

Distribute these cards among the buyers by hand, mail or what have you. (They could very well accompany an announcement of a new product or taking on a new line, for example.)

Bingo Cards

The rep who doesn't appreciate and use these magazine printed request enquiries to the fullest extent, ought to find himself some other occupation. When a man goes to the trouble of filling out and mailing one of these cards, isn't that prima-facie evidence of his interest, that he is a possible customer? And consider how many advertising dollars it cost to produce each card.

Okay – so, at a glance, you recognize some of them are worthless. A few may call for immediate action – by personal call or by phone. But what about the rest? Are they laid aside, to "someday" do something about them like, maybe, if you "happen to be in the neighborhood"? If you have some "spare time"?

That time element! Calculate how long it took before the card was received by the magazine from which it was taken, the time it took to mail it to the manufacturer for whom it was intended, and finally the period elapsing before it was forwarded to you. Then if, in turn, you allow an appreciable length of time to pass before you contact the man who filled out the card in the first place, his interest has become pretty cold, if he hasn't forgotten it altogether.

Admittedly, you can't do anything much about shortening up getting these cards to you, but at least you can do your part in giving them some immediate attention. (You *could* admonish your factories not to be laggard in shooting these out to you – sometimes their own people don't realize the need for forwarding these things promptly.) Have on hand prepared form letters, one for each line. This should identify you, tie you in with the line; you offer to be of assistance, maybe include your line roster and brief reference to your other lines. Such a letter should go out *the very day* you receive the card. I can testify from personal experience, letters of this kind are most productive in getting responses from possible customers.

An idea from Paul Muni

I sometimes think it would be an eye-opener if a person would make a recording of, say, the main portion of his sales pitch. What a revelation it might provide when played back! How some of us would hear, as our listeners do, the boring repetition of the same phraseology, the dwelling on minor details, the meandering, lack of order in presenting key facts.

We all know teachers use such recordings in the course of

analyzing and improving verbal delivery. You might give the same idea a try, say, recording one of your regular sales pitches in privacy, with no one else present. Then, later, have someone else listen to it with you, to comment, to criticize.

The usage of such a procedure is not without professional precedent. Back in the days when I was a distributor, I had an unusual customer in the person of the late Paul Muni, one of the country's finest actors. As an illustration of his earnest artistry: it was his practice to buy a batch of blank recording disks whenever he had an important scene to play. In the privacy of his home, he would first try a number of different ways in which he might do the part, recording each variation. The next day, at the studio, he and his director would go over the recordings, to select and finalize on the presentation which sounded like the best way to do it.

Give your spiel a try – it's always fun to hear your own voice, and – could be very illuminating!

Stockholders' Reports

Aside from investing for profit, (to be discussed in further detail later) owning only a few shares of stock in your principal's company can give you a variety of authentic, very interesting information about the people you represent which you would not learn otherwise. It is mandatory that "public" corporations issue periodical reports to all stockholders. These include official financial statements which can be quite illuminating. Chief officers make detailed reports on the year's progress (or lack of it!), discuss future plans and so on, which you can compare with your actual experience.

Not only that, but you let your sales manager know that you have "bought in" to the company. It makes points in your favor; by risking your own money, you show faith in their prospects, that you are "a member of the family." They like that.

Poor Practices

Factories have been known to make goofs. What of the rep who, when such a mishap occurs, cusses out the factory *to the customer* for being so incompetent, such a bunch of nincompoops and so on? That's pretty bad selling. In his attempts to absolve himself from responsibility, he brings up the inferential thought that, if those people are such jerks, how come he is selling such a lousy line? That kind of rep is just condemning himself.

A very small line that you carry simply because it doesn't take much work but does pay a few bucks, can be a serious detriment. Just the fact that it appears in your roster may stop a sales manager from offering you a similar but really important line because he feels you already have a competitive line. Plus, the longer your roster, the more apt you are to raise questions in the prospective principal's mind about how much time you could devote to his line.

Don't dwell on what one customer is doing in conversation with another. It may cause him to consider you a gossip, that you will also probably be carrying tales to his competitors about what *he* is doing.

If you have terminated with a line, don't knock the products or its personnel afterwards to customers. You may get the buyer to wondering how come you were selling that line in the first place and it sets up doubt in his mind about you. And, as *has* happened, circumstances may occur to bring about your taking the line on again at some future time. Besides, "knocking" is always poor business.

A curious but common failing in even long experienced

salesmen is reluctance to come right out and *ask for the order.* You've given the buyer all you've got. Every point seems to be settled – and still, he procrastinates. He mumbles something about maybe he should take another look at what your competitor has to offer . . . his budget is kinda low . . . he's a slow thinker . . . his mind may be on bettering his golf score next weekend . . . maybe if he keeps you on the anxious seat, he'll extract more concessions – Maybe this, maybe that. . . .

It's surprising how many salesmen diffidently allow themselves to be put off by a buyer who has no hard-and-fast reason for further delay, who only needs a firm, determined prodding to make him act. He knows what you are there for – is frankly *asking* for the order going to stop you from getting it? If nothing else, by putting him right on the spot, you'll bring out any possible *real* reason he may have for turning you down again. More likely, at this point, you'll get the order simply by *asking for it.*

43
SO YOU WANT TO GROW

"I'm not hungry – I just want
to get rich, that's all."

How often have you scoffed at the books that tell you how to make money? Who hasn't asked, if the author knows so much about it, why isn't he himself a millionaire?

Of course! And certainly, this writer has no intention of insulting your intelligence with some kind of a sure-fire "system" for guaranteeing success in the rep business. But, it happens. We do know men who make it big. A fair question would be, however, how do *they* do it? And – what have they got that the average rep hasn't got? Is the *only* answer "big" lines?

I was plugging along, with a pretty fair roster of lines, getting no place fast.

I felt like a sardine packed into a sea of humanity.

I wanted to break out, to be a whale.

Lunching one day with a retired rep friend, I put the question to him:

"What do I have to do to grow in this business? I'm putting in my time, I'm making a living, but what do I do to make money – real money? What's the secret?"

"Depends largely on what you don't do."

"Translation, please?"

He went into a lot of words to say, acquiring know-how is only the beginning, but not enough. He waxed eloquent, with fist-pounding emphasis on the fact that the average rep doesn't follow all the procedures which experience makes familiar through the years. When he got to dwelling on such commonplace things as "frequent mailings, reading trade magazines," and so on, I interrupted with:

"Yeah, sure, I know all that – but who can do all those things within the limitations of 24-hour days?"

He shrugged. "About that, I wouldn't know. I always worked by the job, myself – not by the hour."

He kept on like that, but it was all repetitious. Afterwards, I asked myself – how come these old timers who have it made always talk like the Horatio Alger hard-work-and-application-makes-success stories I used to read when I was a kid?

But I kept thinking about it. I recalled several men I had known who were not brain prodigies, who hadn't been blessed with some particularly lucky break, just ordinary guys, plodding hard workers who, nevertheless, became the outstanding ones in their chosen occupations. For instance, there was this rep who had a promising group of lines but in a thin, geographically widespread territory. To fully develop them would take far more manpower than he had available. He dreaded taking on the costs, the burdens and the problems of hiring additional salesmen. Certainly, a familiar enough situation. So, what did this genius do?

He fell back on one of the oldest, tried-and-true methods for covering a territory, i.e., the mails. From a modest start, he built up a bigger and bigger mailing list, until it ran into thousands of names. He bought a good duplicating machine and studiously followed a vigorous, twice-a-month routine – issuing a constant stream of bulletins, brochures, calling attention to some special product, and so on. He kept hammering away. And as the list grew, so did his business. It developed into a multi-office organization, to become one of the biggest rep operations in the country – all stemming from a comprehensive, steady mailing program.

"Too busy!"

What words are so characteristic of the rep business?

"I'm killing myself, working 12 to 14 hours a day.... Can't afford a good secretary ... Can't keep up with the paper work ... Can't get a decent salesman ... The phone drives me nuts, with all this work I've got to do in the office ... Too many principals in town ... Too many shows...."

Familiar? Who hasn't used the same "explanations" for his lack of progress? Sure, I knew how effective mailing procedures can be. Who doesn't? By now, I was well aware of *what* had to be done – but how in the hell did one find the time to do *all* the things which advance a man in the rep business? While munching a hot dog with a rep friend at a convention, I repeated that question to this man after he had told me of an item in a trade magazine which happened to be important news to me, but which I had missed seeing.

He replied that he habitually read the trade publications during lunch, while waiting in the customers' reception foyers, in certain unmentionable rooms and during commercials when he was watching TV at home. He continued in the same vein, telling me that visiting factory men were always put up at those hotels which maintained limousines for carrying guests to and from the airport, sparing him that time-consuming chore. In one special case, calling frequently on a buyer whose office was always filled with salesmen waiting for interviews, and becoming aware that the buyer was at his desk sharply at nine o'clock, he would show up at a quarter of nine, thus allowing him to be the first man in and soon on his way to the next call.

He went on, with various commonplace little time-saving dodges – none at all unusual or hard to think up – except that he used them.

The secrets of making a rep business grow? There aren't any! The two examples just related typify and, as we've been discussing in previous chapters, there are ways and means, but – I'm finding this extraordinarily difficult to put into words, probably because in summarizing, it sounds too damn simple. Well, I suggest you prove it out for yourself.

Ask any of the "big" reps how they got that way. The responses will be pretty much uniform and honest because they really have nothing to hide. They'll tell you know-how is a must, which is taken for granted of course, but that *you have to apply everything you know*. In one form or another the word "apply" will stand out. If there is any secret at all, that is it. The average rep always has an excuse for not utilizing *all* the legitimate, known ways of expanding his business.

I'm afraid all this sounds like moralizing, but if you think you've been wasting your time reading this chapter, I ask only that you put in just a few minutes more by doing this:

Make a list of every single last way, means or procedure that you now know of or ever heard of for legitimately promoting the advancement of a rep business. *Put it in writing – everything*!

Lay the list aside for at least several days, preferably a week or two, long enough for it to get cold. Then – go over your list. Single out the things *you* don't do. Sit back and ask yourself, Why? What's my excuse?

If you're *honest* with yourself (which will be your greatest difficulty) my bet is that you'll find ways and means for getting yourself out of the "average" rut and on your way to the big time. That is, unless you prefer living with your excuses.

44
FUTURE OF THE REP PROFESSION

Comes the revolution – !

This happened several wars ago – back in that period when the world was preoccupied with the mundane processes of life on the home front, during a kind of armistice, you might say, between World War I and World War II. I was engaged in my first electronic enterprise (then known as the "raddio" business) in a hole-in-the-wall store, with a small stock consisting mainly of radio kits and tubes. I was now old enough to have to shave every day instead of just when I had a date.

One fateful day, an elderly gent who had been highly pleased with the results of a kit bought for his son, entered the store and beckoned surreptitiously for me to follow him to a quiet corner. Between watchful glances over his shoulder, he told me how much he admired my enterprise in so youthfully essaying to become a businessman, went on to warn me not to take it too hard, that everyone had to go through these terrible experiences in commercial life, and finally got to the point.

It seemed he had a cousin, a shipping clerk working for one of the country's famous electrical manufacturers. "Now keep this to yourself," he whispered. "My cousin happened to overhear the company's chief engineer talking with a draftsmen and he told me what they were saying. Oh, boy!" My friend drew me closer and hissed into my ear. "It's a revolution! They've developed some kind of a gadget that's *going to do away with all radio tubes*!" My eyes opened wide, my jaw dropped. "Reason I'm passing this on to you is on account you being such a nice young fellow, I felt you ought to know. They're only waiting to get the price down a bit," he went on, "and then – blooey!" He pointed to the tubes on my shelves. "Those things won't be worth the paper they're packed in!"

With a final finger-shaking admonition not to tell anyone I had heard this horrendous news from him, he walked out, leaving me ready to collapse. I stared in dismay at my stock of tubes, representing the major portion of my capital, now so soon to become worthless. That night, my eyes never closed. In the days that followed, each morning I grabbed the newspaper and went through it column after column, searching for reports relating to the earthshaking discovery. When salesmen came to call, I braced for an announcement of the revolution's arrival and I wondered if I should consult a lawyer about bankruptcy proceedings. I began to read the "help wanted" ads.

Back in those years, the radio industry sold annually ninety-some-odd million dollars worth of consumer products (which included radio receivers *as well* as tubes). Since then, domestic manufacturers' sales of electronic tubes alone have increased to an annual sale of $1.25 billion! Today, we know my well-meaning, rumor-mongering informant wasn't entirely talking nonsense in speaking of a revolutionary device to supplant the use of tubes. He was just a bit premature – by a few decades, that is. But despite his dire predictions and the advent of semiconductors, the tube business thrived, continued to grow and grow, as did the entire electronic industry.

Man's ingenuity erupts continually but each upheaval creates only one mountain in an ever-forming range constantly transforming the technology horizon. Down through the years have come a steady succession of extraordinary new products. They may displace or supplement existing devices; nevertheless, the markets for them become correspondingly bigger. And the manufacturers' representatives grow and multiply, and become more affluent because, no matter how technology's devices proliferate, *more and more customers are created thereby*. Once upon a time, selling tubes for somebody's home radio was just about the extent of my business horizon. I lived to see the day when I would sell products destined for a trip to the moon.

What does our crystal ball portend in terms of the future? I envy the lack of temerity, the superb self-confidence of those who loudly promulgate vivid descriptions of a world soon to be changed beyond recognition. Not but that it is happening. Long-standing social structures are being reshaped, our economy-oriented society and traditional governmental processes questioned. We are tossed about in a bewildering vortex of changing values, such as reformations calculated to alleviate pollution and ecology conditions heretofore taken for granted. We are confronted with the irony of assimilating vastly profound, technological developments changing the entire character of daily living, in the midst of the bloodiest century known to man.

It takes tremendous bravado, indeed, to predict what the world will be like in any given future period. With the past now illuminated by the laser of hindsight, one may well wonder who, at the turn of the century, could have foreseen the course of mankind as, in just one instance, transportation progressed from the livery stable to railroads to automobiles to aeroplanes to intra-planet spacecraft – all in the span of one man's lifetime.

More specifically, consider the developments in the growth of one nationally-known manufacturer alone, in this case from bases of electrical equipment to appliances for the home, from industrial controls to industrial automation, from radio to communication systems, from steam turbines to gas turbines and gas jet engines. Came radar, space vehicles, nuclear power – it's no wonder phrases like "the sky is the limit" have become maundering anachronisms. This industrial behemoth divides those of its products most closely associated with electrical living into three groups. Of these, the second largest is the "Consumer Products group." At a 1970 meeting, an officer of the company stated, "Most of the products of this group *were not in existence ten years ago.*"

Nevertheless, one should not be carried away by the magnitude of the future's uncertainties. While taking part in the great movements of the world, of necessity each of us exists in a microcosm of his own. Therein no one need be discouraged from his aims, his goals, any more than did those before us. As always, barring the unlikely possibility of some great, cataclysmic upheaval in our culture, the business portion of the world will conform to the trends, adopting, modifying, converting to the conditions that pertain. One plows determinedly ahead because indecision is the bastard offspring of fear, than which nothing can be more devastating.

Insofar as any man can really foresee, those identified with the sale of technology's products may well look to continuation of a prospering future. At one low spot during the 1970 recession, I attended a trade meeting where the guest speaker was the purchasing head of an industrial manufacturer employing 3,500 people, with purchases aggregating $25 million per year. To the half-hundred reps in his audience, he laced his opinion about the future of business with some pertinent facts:

"We currently buy 16,000 discrete items from about 2,500 suppliers. As their technology and ours develops, we will undoubtedly buy more and more hardware. Not only that but, for many years to come, we will be needing thousands and thousands of replacement items in order to maintain the equipment we sell. So keep calling on us."

It is only natural to look with concern at the possible influence of automation on selling. No doubt, in time some of the commonplace manual services will be altered, perhaps more centralized. An example might be that of responding to a request for a catalog by a pushbutton procedure leading, in seconds, to the automated delivery of a "hard copy" of the publication by the manufacturer himself, rather than by the rep. Yet, should that come about, it will take a salesman to turn that prospect into a customer ... Some sales person might precede the catalog request by inspiring the prospective interest that generated the desire for more information .... It would take a salesmen to sell the equipment required for such communication. ...

Yes, industrial products do proliferate. But even while the much vaunted wonders of the computer await the device that will foil the ingeniousness of those who will inevitably find means for cheating its readouts, the markets for prosaic, utilitarian items continue to expand. Be they termed hardware, software, or peripheries, pushbuttons, electro-mechanical contraptions or wire – the need for the bolts and nuts of industry is basic at every stage of automation. And with that, men to sell the components from which machines are manufactured, will be required to fulfill the traditional salesman's function of bridging the gap between manufacturer and buyer.

From ocean-bottom to the moon – and beyond

With all the technological developments characterizing major industries, none of them, not even plastics, approaches the influence, the pervasive presence of electronics in our daily lives. The independent professional salesman plays an important role in this fantastic industry, whose annual sales volume at the domestic manufacturers' level exceeds $25 billion. From instrumentation systems to the ubiquitous transistor radio, from the electronic equipment of the huge 747 aeroplane in itself heavier than the total weight of a 707 commercial plane, from one imagination-staggering development to another, electronics continues its spectacular growth, in which the rep is a prominent factor.

As in other major industries, the manufacturers' representative performs a key function in the interlocking interests of supplier and user. But the size of the technical products market now is such that limitations to selected segments must necessarily follow. The so-called "industrial" rep is confronted with the requirements of automation, laser, microcircuitry, computer peripheries, electromedical equipment, geophysics, optics, data processing, scientific research, educational devices, holography, process control, nucleonics, noise, shock, vibration and pollution control – the list goes on and on. Nor does this include the rep who deals in "consumer products," in home entertainment and business needs, in commercial sound, in the innumerable variations of record players, hi fi, radios, television, cassettes, appliances, burglar alarms and accessories, in a market potentially without limits because *everybody* is a consumer of sorts!

I cannot close this chapter without reference to the moments of discouragement with which reps often sit back, contemplating the problems accompanying the never-ending new outputs of technology. Some years ago, a rep friend of mine, operating a small firm with a few employees, had attended a university seminar devoted to discussing the electronic industry. There he listened somberly to academic speculation on the effects of oncoming automation, of discrete parts to be eliminated – "a thousand transistors on the head of a pin" – and the like. He returned to his business in a depressed mood. "I wonder what, if anything, we'll be selling two or three years from now," he sighed.

Well, it may be pins, but I doubt it. He must be selling something more because as of this writing, he has sixteen people in his organization and he is still repping electronics.

No, it is not within the ken of this writer or anyone else to make hard and fast predictions of what the future holds for manufacturers' representation. One can only note that the products of modern day industry are used from the very bottom of the earth's oceans on up into boundless, outer space.

What a territory for an ambitious rep to work!

45
ANTICIPATING RETIREMENT

For the oddball who prefers
fishing, golfing and homelife to
sales manager, expediters and secretaries

I am not presumptuous enough to assume the role of financial counsellor, attorney, accountant, banker, wife or any of such pros whom you should consult in thinking about retirement. But I do have a point to make: while there are many roads to financial security, you've got to get cracking – you've got to start setting up a retirement program *while you're still working for a living* – and that isn't as pointless as it may sound.

It helps to be lucky but, just as in the case of this writer and so many others, you don't have to be a genius to retire. To many men, being all through with the exigencies of business life is remote. So is the moon. But reaching your Eldorado, your planet of affluence, is not all that far away, *providing* you anticipate, prepare! You have to do the astronaut bit with blueprints, with take-off platforms. Putting it another way: *specific plans for your future are the molds for jelling dreams into realization.*

Ask the still youngish man, say in his forties, what plans he has for retiring from the grinding away of everyday business life. The response is seldom anything more than a big, sighing, "some day" – so far away there isn't any use even thinking about it. But as any older man can testify, in terms of time, "far away" sneaks up on you and all of a sudden the future becomes the present and by tomorrow it's your past.

Well – so what about those "plans," those concrete steps to take? What are they? Hell's fire – don't ask me – how should I know? As I said in the beginning, you go to the pros for drawing up your specifics. But – this I do know – a balloon full of wishes isn't going to get you off the ground. You may still be only a small operation but, if your business is reasonably well established, if you're doing a bit better than just making a living, it's time to begin planning *your* trip to the moon.

Not that we're going to even try to arrive at any conclusions here, but let's kick things around a bit. What, generally speaking, will you discuss with your pros? No doubt, the process of how to dispose of your business when you are ready to retire, becomes an initial subject. For reasons all too obvious, selling a rep business is almost out of the question. "Almost," that is. Because you should have one ready, built-in prospective buyer, willing and anxious to take over.

Before becoming involved in that phase of the situation, I suggest you arm yourself with a figure which should be a most significant base for your calculations. In short: what scale of living do you look forward to in retirement? I don't mean the life of a millionaire because if that's what you're thinking of, you might as well throw this book away. For miracles, I'm afraid you'll have to look Higher Up. I'm asking, in practical terms, what would you settle for in the way of a realistic figure?

Let's discuss that for a moment. Have you ever tried to compute *exactly* how much per year you would *really* need to live on without working? Say within a thousand dollars or so? If you haven't, it will be something of a revelation to learn how much *less* you'll need than you think.

Get out your records of living expenses – by receipts, checkbook or what have you. List all your regular, built-in expenditures, one by one, say, for several years back. Delete items which, in advancing age, aren't likely to come up again, such as big-ticket items for your home, the kind of expenses which you won't have if you're not in business and so on. Take an average yearly total. (Allow an estimate for major contingencies – perhaps an investment gone sour or a major pleasure trip.) Assume that total is your income. Compute how much lower your income tax would be on that amount than it is at present, but add that in. (Think of how many months out of the year you work now, just to make enough to pay your current income tax!)

The underlying point to keep in mind here is that it's not what your resources are worth after you retire – it's the amount of *spendable income* they produce that counts. If you accept the fact that "life is a series of compromises," the results of the foregoing simple mathematics will make it evident that you can retire and get along just as well as you do now but with a lot less income needed.

So, looking forward to the kids grown up and on their own, just you and the wife and inflation to consider, you've fixed a reasonable but fairly definite annual amount on which you could retire. Using that figure as a starter, you do some multiplying: what, in intrinsic resources, will it take to produce that much income? With such a "master" figure in the background of your mind, now you and your pros have something in the nature of a definite target at which to aim. We'll refer to that again later, but in the meantime –

Let's say that, at this time, you're too far down the road for long-range planning. You've become a well known, firmly established, highly regarded company. But, you're tired; you're feeling the weight of your years: you'd like to quit. Now, that business in which you invested so many years of blood, sweat and tears – you'd like to sell out and go fishing.

In one way, it's more difficult to get out of business than to get into it. If you've waited this long, you're at a big disadvantage. Based on the amount of income your business is producing, as compared to other economic enterprises, your business should be worth a huge sum of money. And it is – but nobody is going to give you that much for it. What you'd like to sell doesn't have tangible, visible worth. Sales agreements aren't salable. Good will has no fixed or easily transferred value. And any prospect who has that kind of money, doesn't need to go into business. You've got a tough problem on your hands – your own fault because you waited so long. But if, by any chance, an opportunity should arise for making a straight, across-the-counter sale of the business, a common approach to establishing its price is to multiply your average annual "take" by perhaps three to five years preceding the sale. You should get more, But – !

There could be another remote possibility, likewise a long shot. You might find a man who wants to get into the rep business, has some substantial capital, and doesn't care to put in the long years necessary by starting from scratch. Perhaps he could be induced to pay you for a partnership, you agreeing to shift total ownership over to him over a pre-determined period of time at a fixed amount or percentage.

A much more likely approach is to seek out an established rep and offer to merge your two operations. Generally speaking, the attraction to the other fellow is that overnight he would have a business hugely increased in size which, by virtue of your retirement arrangement, would ultimately be all his.

The most probable and common way is to sell out to your employees. If you have good salesmen, chances are they are of your breed – individualistic, ambitious to be in business for themselves. They're enterprising, anxious for the chance to be "head man," the kind of unique men drawn to the rep business. They are already familiar with your business, know the lines, the potentialities – you have only to agree on the terms. But for that, you should have planned long ago, which is what I am trying to tell you!

We'll be getting back to that. But let's digress, momentarily, and take a look at a couple of other roads leading to your goals.

Manufacturers' representation is a good business but if you're going to depend *entirely* on repping to provide your retirement income, you're quite an optimist. It's been done – but it's more realistic to supplement your rep earnings with other activities or investments.

Too common to discuss, quite standardized, desirable and comparatively simple is, of course, income real estate. What you may not understand about it is easily checked through your bank and brokers, by way of supplementing your own judgment of a property's worth. You don't even have to wait to accumulate large sums for down payments; arrangements for individuals with small money to join groups buying big income properties are now commonplace . . . . Some of the insurance people have plans you should look into. . . .

But what about the stock market? Now, hold it! Don't throw up your hands with a "Hell,no!" Too many reps overlook the fact that, "ex post officio," they are in a particularly advantageous, opportune position, sometimes even better qualified under certain circumstances to judge a security's worth than some of the people who make an occupation of it! That's a money-making fact which I learned rather accidentally.

It started as a joke. I was still repping, when all "stock market" meant to me was the smells assailing my nostrils during attendance at conventions in Chicago. One of the accounts I had been calling on was a small outfit, engaged in research and light production of a device which, in this manufacturer's dreams, had potential for a multi-million-dollar enterprise.

One day, while having lunch with one of their rather verbose, top men, something led him to talking about a friend of his who, though supposedly a shrewd investor, had bought some of this company's stock despite its highly speculative nature. "I guess that at 1-1/8, the guy figured he couldn't lose much," he chuckled.

Not that I was interested but, to make conversation, I asked what "1-1/8" meant. He explained this stood for a cost of $1.12 per share. "Oh," I said and, bored, changed the subject to his people's prospects for getting a huge order he had been hinting about. That kind of language I understood!

Some time later, I took an order from them for 10,000 pieces of a small item, of which only one was used in each of their devices. The following day, they gave me an order for a kind of equipment which I knew would be required only for big production. This began to add up – the important, prospective customer must have come through! They were on their way!

I got to thinking about that stock thing. That night, I said to my wife, "I'm going to buy 100 shares of this company's stock. We'll put it away in the deposit box and some day we'll wake up and find we're millionaires! And if not – what the hell – it's only a hundred and some bucks – if we lose it, we can still eat." Delighted with the prospect of becoming a millionaire, she agreed.

The next day, she called a stock broker with whom we had some slight acquaintance, to tell him we wanted to buy 100 shares of stock in the outfit. He had never heard of them. It took some time before he gathered the data before him. Whereupon he said to her:

"My dear – why don't you get that husband of yours to take you to Las Vegas and have some fun for your money? This is just throwing it away!"

But I had previously alerted her to expect such a reaction and, so, we acquired the stock. And, it went up and up. I kept buying more, until I had five hundred shares. Eventually, I sold out at a nice profit. But *that* is not the point of the story.

Each time the broker was called to repeat buying more of the same stock for us, he commented on its rise and added that I "must have had some good information." Which indeed I did. Which awakened me to the fact that in the course of calling on industrials big enough to be "public," the rep acquires most meaningful information about them. The same applies to his principals; the rep frequently gains significant *inside* knowledge of a company's potentialities, of the kind of management they have, of the progress they can be expected to make.

As I began timidly to buy more stocks in various corporations with which I was familiar – but only customers and principals – and saw my judgment verified by their increased worth, I learned that the "experts" consider this kind of insight of tremendous value in judging just what to buy or sell, and when. (As a matter of fact – and this really gave us the giggles – that same stock broker got to calling *me* at times, asking me *my* opinion in connection with various electronic stocks!)

I'm not suggesting that you become a "trader" in the stock market. Heaven forbid! The daily financial reports give ample evidence of how frequently the supposedly most knowledgeable men become confounded in their trading activities. What I am pointing up is that you could consider *conservatively* investing solely in companies with which *you* are intimately familiar. And even then – don't put money out *unless you can afford to lose it* because, under the most favorable of circumstances, *no one* is an infallible prophet when it comes to the stock market!

In my case, I had some losses – sure! If you keep at it, it's inevitable – you're bound to get hooked! But, as it happened, I figured right more times than wrong, and so I made out. In fact, when an opportunity arose to make a good buy in the form of a real estate property, it was the profits I made on my stocks that enabled me to swing the deal. It couldn't have been done on my rep earnings alone.

Well, back to the most likely routes for getting out of your business. Consider merging with another rep firm, which is the same thing as going into partnership. Joining forces with the other fellow can be an entirely pragmatic course to follow or, let's face it, as I said before about partnerships, the outcome may turn out to be a togethermess. The philosophical implications of clashing temperaments, of varying approach to business methods, as well as line conflicts, are uppermost possibilities for making this a thorny way to go. But, the manifest advantages make it worth every consideration.

As possibilities for merging, you study the firms with which you have some familiarity and, after deletions for obvious reasons, in all probability you are looking at a very narrow list. Comparative size has great bearing, naturally. If Firm A is bigger than yours (best authenticated by comparing financial statements for the preceding three years), your share of the combination will make you a minor partner. In actual effect, you become a high echelon employee, your main value being that you bring to the new organization a list of desirable lines.

Or, if Firm A is smaller than you, of course, exactly the reverse is true. Either situation is practicable, providing one of you is willing to be submerged to the other in order to carry out your plans. Since the intent is for you to retire in a comparatively short term, this should not be too great a barrier.

Assume your business is substantial enough for you to be in a favorable negotiating position. In the course of reaching agreement, you work up the details of when and who gets how many of the dollars involved. You take care of the lines' conflict possibilities. Now the principals: their acquiescence in the passing over of the lines shouldn't present difficulties because first, you are still on the job and your withdrawal is going to be a kind of sub-rosa, gradual process. In addition, they will welcome the prospect of increased manpower repping them. A very decided advantage of merging is that if the terms of your retirement include payments to you over a prolonged period of time, the larger the firm you plan to leave behind, the more likely will be the assurance of its continued prospering existence and that you will be paid out.

If ultimate selling out and retirement is still a long-range prospect, as you hire salesmen, no matter what you pay them or the remuneration terminology, determine that an important portion be in the form of periodical, increasing ownership in your company. Impress your presumed "buyer-outer" with the realization that some day he is going to be the owner, or one of them, of your business. (If such a proposition doesn't appeal to him, you can assume he isn't going to stay with you!)

Note this: if your plans call for eventually selling the business to your employees, you have to start with one basic condition, the ironic fact that, in effect, *you* have to provide them with the means for buying you out. That's the way it indeed is.

Broadly generalized, what that means is issuing ownership shares to your prospective "buyer-outer," spaced out over the years while he is in your employ or, perhaps, periodically depositing cash sums for him to use when the time comes for taking over your keys to the place.

Naturally, the big problem is going to be establishing a formula to cover percentages of compensation and time relevancy, whether by stock or some IRS-blessed cash depositary method. A start might be the target number of years you estimate to reach your retirement point. Decide on the percentage of ownership which you contemplate the men having by that time. Divide the number of years by the proportionate amount of interest each one is to receive annually, to reach that final percentage of ownership. While you might consider the possibility of retaining a life-long interest in the company, it would be preferable to make your deal some version of a finalized sale, fixed on you getting out altogether (particularly if you feel uncertain about how the business will be handled with you no longer at the helm). Obviously, the variances in individual circumstances make it impossible for anyone save you and your advisors to spell out the specifics of this procedure.

You and your pros will have much to think about and discuss. How about pensions, out of your business or in conjunction with the plans offered by leading insurance companies? What kind of a combination or balance of pensions, outside investments and proceeds from the sale of your business should you look for to provide that "master" figure which you established as a target on which you could retire? How will you stand on taxes?

At this point, if the possibility of retiring is still far off, you may be thinking all this meandering, hopping about among different procedures, is meaningless, crystal ball stuff. Why waste time trying to look ahead to what the continually changing conditions will be like in the long years to come? Who has that kind of foresight in this tumultuous world?

Okay – so let's say your guesstimating couldn't possibly be accurate. We can be pretty sure, it won't be – you can't control *all* the things that are going to happen to you. But – if, with professional assistance, you've drawn up a reasonably well thought out assembly of plans, you can vary them from time to time as circumstances dictate, can't you – suiting them to the conditions as they may develop? At least, you will have definite guide lines to follow, even though you might have to branch off here or there. I only know that the day will come when you will wake up, when conditions make it desirable, even necessary that you quit the business world. All of a sudden, you're going to be asking yourself, How do I get out?

Which brings me to the whole sum, substance and total of this chapter – my hope that you will get off the dime, stop procrastinating and head straight for the pros, to map the routes that will put you on the right road to retirement.

Happy Travelling!